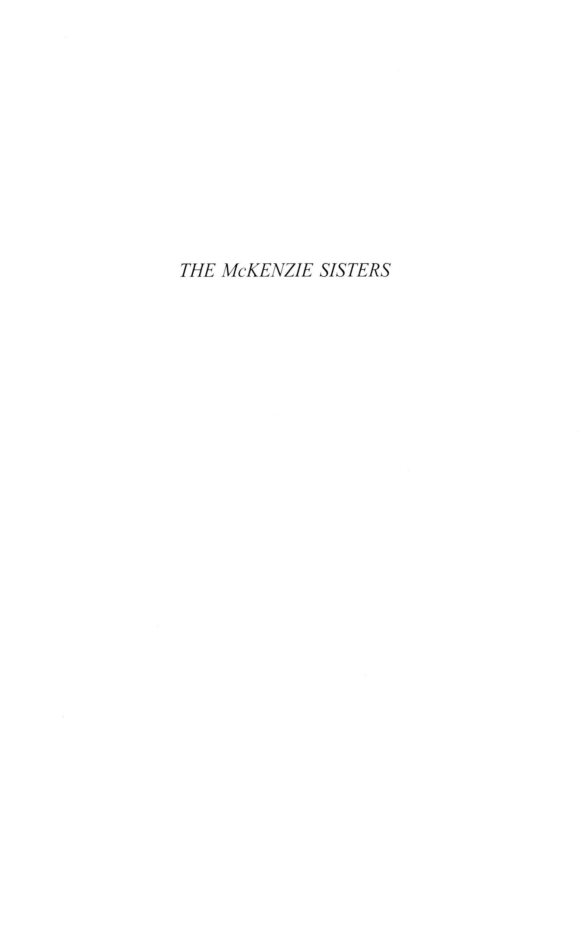

THE McKENZIE SISTERS

Bookplate designed for Winifred and Alison
By their friend Jozef Sekalski A.R.E.

The McKenzie Sisters

The lives and art of Winifred and Alison McKenzie
With 16 monochrome photographs & illustrations, 13 colour plates
A foreword by David McClure, and two reviews by Edward Gage

Aylwin Clark

BLACK ACE BOOKS

© Aylwin Clark and Winifred McKenzie 1996
Foreword © David McClure 1996

Typeset in Scotland by Black Ace Editorial
Ellemford, Duns, Berwiskhire, TD11 3SG

Printed in England by Redwood Books
Kennet Way, Trowbridge, Wilts, BA14 8RN

A CIP catalogue record for this book
is available from the British Library

ISBN   1–872988–51–2

Acknowledgements

We would like to acknowledge with special gratitude the kindness which led Dr James Macaulay, Senior Lecturer in the Glasgow School of Art, University of Glasgow, to undertake research into the early records of the Glasgow School of Art and to give us information about George McKenzie as a student.

Warmest thanks also to Ann Simpson, Librarian at the Gallery of Modern Art in Edinburgh, who first floated the suggestion that the McKenzie sisters had never been written up, and to Vanessa Prosser, who seized upon the idea and encouraged us to realize it.

Otto Macaig in Monmouth has been consistently helpful and co-operative on any query we have raised with him; his friendship with Winifred goes back fifty years now to wartime St Andrews.

The publishers are grateful to the *Scotsman* for permission to reproduce the reviews by Edward Gage in Chapter 13.

CONTENTS

Foreword by David McClure RSA RSW RGI   10

Introduction by Winifred McKenzie   13

CHAPTERS

1   George McKenzie: His Bombay Childhood and
    Scottish Schooling, 1866–84   15

2   The Profession of Architecture, 1884–9   18

3   Life in Bombay, 1889–96   32

4   Marriage, 1896–1913   37

5   Kilmacolm, 1913–23   46

6   Glasgow School of Art, 1923–30   52

7   London, 1930–40   62

8   The First Impact of War, 1939–40   70

9   The War Years for Winifred, 1940–5   78

10   The War Years for Alison, 1940–6   88

11   Dundee College of Art, 1944–57   94

12   Back to Painting, 1957–66   99

13   Full Steam Ahead, 1966–84, including two
    Scotsman reviews by Edward Gage   103

Appendix: Books for Reference   112

List of 15 Plates following   113

Photographs & Illustrations

Winifred at eighty-eight   12

The McKenzie Family   14

The Boating Party, with Charles Rennie Mackintosh   17

George with his Fiat in Bombay   31

The Little Mem-sahib: Winifred with her ayah and boy   35

George with his Family   36

Mary McKenzie with her Daughters   44

Silhouette of Mary McKenzie with her Violin   45

Alison's Free Photograph   60

Winifred's Free Photograph   61

Winifred with Annabel Kidston   77

The Woodcut Monty Saw: Newbattle Abbey   93

On Holiday with Violette Dufour   98

Friends of the RSA in Paris   102

To the memory of George McKenzie,
Father of Winifred and Alison.

The discovery of his diary led on,
through the reviving of memories,
to the writing of this work.

Foreword

Aylwin Clark's biography of the McKenzie sisters is perceptive, vivid and entertaining. The history of their family makes fascinating reading, as do the recollections by Winifred of their days at Glasgow School of Art.

The McKenzie sisters came to the opening of my first solo exhibition in Aitken Dott's, then situated in Castle Street, Edinburgh, in 1957. They were very encouraging. The works in this exhibition were the result of my two years as Andrew Grant Fellow at Edinburgh College of Art. The first part of my study was drawing and painting landscape on the Isle of Cumbrae in the Firth of Clyde. The second part was work done in Italy and Sicily. I felt I had not found a personal voice then, but perceptive comments by Winifred and Alison were of great help to me, and this indicated to me that, like many gifted artists, they were inspiring teachers, and I am grateful.

The other thing I have to thank them for is that when they were retiring from teaching at Dundee College of Art, it meant that a full-time post was created and they drew my attention to it and invited me over from Edinburgh to look round the Art College. I was introduced to Hugh Adam Crawford, the Principal, and to Alberto Morrocco, Head of Drawing and Painting. I was subsequently given the post; so that I got a job which gave me a sound foundation to continue to practise as a painter.

The expression 'less is more' is (like most aphorisms) only part-truth. Sometimes 'more' *is* 'more' and sometimes 'less' is simply 'less'. But in the work of Winifred and Alison their individual ways of simplifying their subjects – whether of objects or the natural world – are never empty of content; rather they intensify meaning and matter and thus intensify our view of things. Pondering upon the imagery in the work of both sisters, one is reminded that painting, print-making, drawing, etc, are a language and that every language has its grammar and syntax. But beyond grammar and syntax there is this: that "if language was the result of logic, not of poetry, we would have only one."

One could be forgiven for thinking of the lives and works of Winifred and Alison as a unique kind of 'blend'. On closer inspection and observation we find they are in fact two distinct 'single malts'; each with her own personal flavour, colour, texture and tone.

I was first introduced to them – at the show I mentioned above – by Anne Redpath, and there are parallels in her work and theirs; the subtle use of tones, gradations, and textures of whites, and the insistence on form and structure in a painting or print as an essential element and virtue. The McKenzie sisters stand for all that is good in art and in life. They encouraged the young. They have a great circle of friends and admirers. Their work and sisterhood have given us all great joy.

David McClure
June 1996

Winifred at 88

Introduction

This biography evolved when Aylwin came to my rescue, after I had had a spell in hospital, by staying with me to allow me to recover at home.

My father's diary had just been discovered and had fascinated us both, and Aylwin suggested we should go on with the McKenzie story.

Family circumstances had obliged my father to give up his career as an architect and return to India, where he died while his daughters were still children, I being only seven and Alison two years younger. He would have been delighted had he known that his daughters had spent their lives together as painters.

My convalescence was greatly helped by recalling the past for Aylwin to write up. We both thoroughly enjoyed these sessions and hope that this story may be of some interest to others.

Winifred McKenzie
St Andrews, June 1996

The McKenzie Family

Standing (from left to right): Harry, Madge, Alexander McKenzie (George's father). *Seated:* George, Alex, Georgina McKenzie (George's mother), Kenneth, Charles, Mary.

Harry became an eye specialist; Madge married and became Mrs Dunk; Alex lived in Helensburgh and had a woollens factory; Kenneth joined his father's Bombay firm later, having married Amy Osborne, George's sister-in-law; Charles went into the Indian Forestry Commission and married Amy Sangster; who, after Charles' death, lived in the Tower of Glenstrae, Loch Awe; Mary married Alec Turner and lived in Jersey.

1

George McKenzie: His Bombay Childhood

And Scottish Schooling, 1866–84

George was the eldest son of Alexander McKenzie, who came from near Glasgow. As a boy Alexander was sent to France to learn about cabinet making, French polishing and allied crafts. When he returned to Glasgow and his uncle's workshop, he asked for an increase in salary in recognition of this training – and he was refused. This seemed grossly unfair to McKenzie with his strong sense of justice and love of straight dealing. He also had a quick temper, so there were no negotiations: he threw up his job in his uncle's firm and headed for India – in a sailing vessel round the Cape of Good Hope, a voyage which would have taken him well over two months.

He landed in Bombay and found a job with a firm concerned with supplying building materials. But when he discovered that the firm was selling substandard bricks and pointed this out to his employers, he was given the sack. This time, determined to be his own master, he started a saw mill, which became a flourishing business. He married Georgina Rose, the daughter of an Army officer, in Bombay and was steadfast, for the rest of his life, in his affection for and admiration of his wife. His granddaughters, Winifred and Alison, found that he had written in the family Bible for the benefit of his children:

'After this book, may thoughts of your Mother guide you.'

All that Winifred remembers of her grandmother is of a little, gentle, white-haired figure at Crieff Hydro, welcoming them in the morning, when she and Alison, still very small, would go along to her room and climb into her bed and she would give them tiny square HP biscuits, which they relished as special – though they probably left as many crumbs as ordinary biscuits!

George John, born on 5 August 1866 in Bombay, was the first of seven children: five boys and two girls. Of all of them, he was the one with the most go. Later his brother Ken said to Winifred and Alison:

'George was special.'

His mother had a neat way of showing her assessment of her sons, George and Harry, when she observed:

'You could give Harry a pair of scissors and know it would be put only to orthodox use but George would think of a hundred ways to have fun with his pair.'

But he had to bear the brunt of parental wrath. On one occasion his father actually knocked him senseless. Alexander conformed, in fact, to the pattern of the Victorian father: authoritarian, energetic; benevolent. He not only built up and ran a profitable business, he was an enthusiastic member of the Free Masons in Bombay and was made Grand Master of their Lodge. He also became head of the YMCA in Bombay, while his wife was involved in running the YWCA. He wanted all his children to be well educated – which meant, in his view, their being sent back to Britain. Again it was the eldest who bore the brunt of trial and error with regard to schools. Their parents decided on a school in Helensburgh – Larchfield – when George reached that stage. George's chief memory of his school days was of bleak holidays in empty buildings when George and Harry were left on their own: cold, echoing corridors and wholly inadequate heating, which meant very painful chilblains, another vivid memory of their earliest days in Scotland.

The Boating Party

George McKenzie is on the left, Charles Rennie Mackintosh on the right. George and Mackintosh were in the same year at the Glasgow School of Art and became friends. At one time the two of them, with John Keppie, hoped to become partners as architects, but this fell through when George was summoned back to India by his father.

2

The Profession of Architecture, 1884–9

It was in 1884, when he was eighteen, that George enrolled at the
Glasgow School of Art to start training, as his father had done,
as a cabinet maker. He seems to have been living in lodgings,
because his first address in Old Dumbarton Road was crossed
out in the School's records and another, in Renfrew Street, was
substituted. The School at that time was in 'its makeshift home in
the Corporation Galleries where classes had been held for nearly
thirty years'.

Makeshift the premises may have been, but the School itself was
full of life: ideas and achievements abounded in art and architecture, especially after the arrival in 1885 of 'Fra' Newbery, (Francis
Newbery, 1854–1946) as headmaster. He was only thirty-one, an
Englishman and a painter, who had taught at South Kensington
and came to Glasgow fully aware of what was significant in
contemporary British and European art and architecture, and with
a new curriculum which offered 'a complete cycle of Technical,
Artistic Education, applicable to the Industrial Arts of the City
of Glasgow'. He proved to be a superb teacher and administrator
and, while being a strict disciplinarian, encouraged his students to
develop their own individuality.

George McKenzie's response was enthusiastic: he took up
painting and gained prizes both in 'model and freehand drawing' (1885) and for 'design for a painted panel' (1886) in a
national competition. Only two of his paintings survive: one
of green woods and water, the other shimmering with Indian
heat. Both fill one with regret that he could not have developed
his talent.

It was part of the philosophy of the Glasgow School of Art under

Newbery that a painter should be involved in architecture as well as art, and George wanted to equip himself to earn his living and was looking forward to marrying and raising a family. So, in 1886, according to the records of the School, he apprenticed himself to an architect and began to study his new profession. It meant dividing his time between School and office: as he wrote in his 1889 diary when he was at Chartres:

'I recognized the originals of some of the plaster casts we have in the office and in the School of Art.'

There is no record of which firm of architects he was articled to but there are various pointers to its being that of Campbell Douglas and James Sellars. John Keppie (architect, 1862–1945) was, at this time Sellars' chief draughtsman, and although four years older than George, had already been on holiday with him in France. In 1889, they decided to go together on a tour of the Loire valley. The friendship may have developed in Sellars' office. It was certainly one which Keppie prized, as he showed when he gave George a signet ring in which he had a cornelian set, with the McKenzie crest on it. It was this ring which Alison wore when she was in the Army and which Winifred still wears today.

Then in 1888 came Glasgow's 'International Exhibition', when Sellars' oriental design for it was chosen by the City Fathers. Keppie and George McKenzie would thus have been fully involved in all the planning of building Glasgow's 'Baghdad by Kelvinside'. George would have felt doubly involved because one of the aims of the Exhibition was to raise enough funding for a new building for the School of Art as well as an Art Gallery and Museum. The Fine Arts section had a sculpture gallery organized by Fra Newbery and a gallery for architectural drawings from all over Britain, which reflected the contemporary vitality of Glasgow's architects. It was generally judged to be one of the departments in which Glasgow surpassed Manchester's earlier exhibition (to do this was an ardent, though unacknowledged, aim of the Glaswegians). A McKenzie family tradition has it that George McKenzie was Clerk of Works at the Exhibition, and this would fit in if he had been with Sellars for his training. Mr Shand, the Chief Clerk of Works, would have been ready to enlist the help of someone Mr Sellars recommended.

In October 1888, however, James Sellars died of blood poisoning (said to have been caused by his treading on a nail on the Exhibition site). Perhaps it was at this point that John Keppie, Charles Rennie Mackintosh and George McKenzie discussed plans for going into partnership together – plans about which George later told his wife and she told Winifred. George and Charles Rennie Mackintosh were in the same year in their architectural course. Mackintosh was the most gifted student in the School and George had won an architectural prize in a national competition, with the Queen's prize for books. They might be natural allies and if the photograph, which Winifred now has, of George in a boat with four others, does indeed include Mackintosh as family tradition believed – then they were ready enough to enjoy themselves together. But Keppie was taken into partnership by John Honeyman and any previous plans were dropped.

That George appreciated Charles Rennie Mackintosh's ideas of design in furniture was shown by his having a set of teak chairs made in India, modelled on Mackintosh's high-backed style, with their strong vertical lines, like the ones in Miss Cranston's tea rooms. After George's death it was the younger son, Ken, who took the chairs to his house in Jersey, but when he died they were sold. Whatever stage George's plans for the future had reached, they were certainly focused in August of 1889 on an architectural career, when he, John Keppie and Hugh McNab planned to go together to explore the châteaux and cathedrals of the lower Seine and Loire valleys and to see for themselves the great Universal Exhibition in Paris. George alone planned to go on after Paris, through Switzerland to Italy.

He kept a diary of these travels of his in the summer of 1889.

It makes refreshing reading: it is vivid, amusing, unaffected and shrewd. It is also a memorial to what might have been a distinguished architectural career.

They had planned to sail from Glasgow at the end of July in the 'William Connal' but were kept hanging about for four days with no explanation or apology for the delay. They finally set out on Saturday. On 3 August George's friend, Bob Wallace, came down to the docks to see them off. (Bob Wallace's sister, Jessie, was later to become George's first wife). Neither the ship nor their own quarters inspired any confidence whatever, especially when the first mate told them in passing that the ship had already foundered three times. With this somewhat risky voyage ahead of them, 'we did one wise thing,' wrote George, 'in seizing the opportunity of not starting for an hour or two, to go and purchase some lemons, biscuits, etc, and a bottle of brandy,' stores they must have been glad of after the wretched, 'greasy-looking stuff' the ship's cook served up to them for dinner. They had another cause of complaint when they found that the ship was going to call at Newport for a cargo of iron rails. But none of them was bothered by seasickness and Hugh McNab was 'not sorry to get a longer sea voyage' as he was not at all well.

To pass the time, George and John Keppie got out their pads and 'made colour sketches of the after-deck of our ship' and they enjoyed having the hose played over them each morning by the huge Irish mate, who would rouse them with a shout of:

'Get up, begorrah! It's six bells and I'll put the hose on yous!'

They had to put in to Cardiff for a pilot to take them up the mouth of the River Usk to Newport, where they found nothing to commend, after they had inspectd 'this dirty, uninteresting place'. They were delayed there a day and a half, which at least gave George the chance to get off his 'Indian letter'. They didn't reach Le Havre till half past eight on Saturday evening – a whole week after they had set out. And 'what a contrast to our last port of call!' George wrote, rejoicing in 'the broad streets with boulevards, squares and gardens and the fine clean appearance' of the place, not to mention their delicious supper ashore. 'How we did relish "le merlan, ragout avec champignons, petits pois avec beurre" and the fromage Roquefort, not to mention the nice bread. We then went to a café and enjoyed one of the Captain's cigars and felt happy.'

That night they sat up on deck, singing and chatting while the ship made its way up the Seine to Rouen, through such pleasing countryside that:

'We wished there were no such places as large cities, with nothing but poverty and dirt.'

The ship's crew were sorry to see the young men go but they were very aware of the time they had lost, so they 'determined to start work at once', revisiting places they had seen before in Rouen, which was like meeting old friends. They pushed on to Evreux and then to Dreux, where they stayed the night. But after inspecting the cathedral they didn't linger, 'on account of the very primitive sanitary arrangements and the second-class quality of things in general.'

Chartres was a different matter altogether. For one thing they were met on their arrival by 'our old friend, Andrew Prentice, who had been travelling in Italy and had come to France to join us in our proposed tour through the Loire district'. (Andrew Prentice had been awarded the Soane Medallion in 1888.) They had an evening of joyous reunion 'comparing notes and asking questions at the Hôtel du Grand Monarque'. The next morning they separated, 'each to study the Cathedral at our leisure', and both of the next two days George went back 'as there is so much to learn in it'. He made a colour sketch of the cathedral and also, in strolling through the town, he drew 'old iron-work door handles, etc'.

Everything about Chartres pleased him, including the food.

On Friday 16 August they went on to Orleans, where George, 'after taking a stroll through the town and making a few notes, went back to the hotel to write my Indian letter' – a duty not to be neglected. They had been told that Orleans was not a town worth visiting but George found its history interesting and understood better than ever before the function of a cathedral as the focus and setting of Catholic worship. When they went on Sunday it proved to be a mass for first communicants, with processions of young women, dressed in white and veiled, led by their priests. The music, the chanting and the solemnity of the occasion, with the bishop 'in a gorgeous red and gold embroidered gown, blessing everyone as he passed', made George grasp 'the full meaning of a Gothic cathedral'.

The next day (Monday 19 August) they were at Blois, where they were all: 'quite delighted with the Château. I had seen photographs of it often,' George went on, 'but they did not lead me to understand it was so rich in all things architectural . . . I have made up my mind to study details only, as they will come in very useful and as we intend buying photographs.' That day they had to say goodbye to Hugh McNab because he had only a three-week break and didn't want to miss Paris.

'Poor McNab', George commented, 'he has not had much of a holiday as he was hardly at any time quite free from his nasty headache.'

The other three, on Tuesday (20 August), hired a trap and drove to Chambord. It proved to be a day of sheer delight: the vineyards and those at work in them, the park in which the Château stood, the Château itself, 'the most beautiful we had ever seen . . . We were quite fascinated by the glorious façade and the irregular, picturesque skyline. We did no work but bought some photographs and walked round the building at least a dozen times . . . The beautifully proportioned and carved dormers don't lose any of their charm from a closer inspection which our ascending to the roof allowed of . . . I shall never forget the pleasant day we spent there and the jolly ride home . . . '

On the Wednesday they got down to work again in the château at Blois: 'Andrew is measuring the whole of the court façade and John is confining himself to making water colours. I have made one water colour but am taking miscellaneous jottings both outside and inside the building . . . '

They left Blois in a deluge of rain on Thursday but the weather cleared and they 'jumped out at Chaumont, just to see the Château', leaving their luggage at the station and crossing the bridge over the Loire, for the half hour's walk to the château. Here they were disappointed to find the Prince was in residence and the restorers at work in a way that provoked the disapproval of these young purists. On the other hand, a great plus for George, who was passionately fond of horses, they could visit the stables. 'They were a treat for us,' he wrote. 'Everything was in as perfect good order as things are on board a man of war. The head groom was very polite and painstaking with us.'

They rejoined the train and spent that Thursday night at Tours. They visited the cathedral but by dinner had decided to leave the next morning. 'There were one or two rather fine courtyards but nothing to the fine courtyards one sees in Italy in photographs, and which it is to be my good fortune to see!' They spent the evening at a Café Chantant and sat down beside an Englishman who turned out to be: 'Briggs the Soane Medallionist of four years ago!' (Robert Alexander Briggs actually won it in 1883.) 'We made friends at once and Briggs decided to go with us to Azay-le-Rideau and after that, on to Paris. He is a very nice fellow,' George went on, 'and is now in practice for himself in London and is over here for a short holiday.'

At Azay-le-Rideau they thought the situation of the château and its simple exterior superb – but the interior: 'the most extravagantly fantastical in its taste. The rooms are all over-decorated and too crowded with not too tasteful furniture; they give one the idea of its belonging to a "Vanderbilt" who has a peacock head.' In spite of these strictures the young men weren't blind to the interesting and useful details there and attacked them with footrules and plummets!

On Saturday (24 August), realizing that Chinon was only half an hour's journey from Azay-le-Rideau, the four of them decided that they must not miss the opportunity of seeing 'one of France's most historically interesting castles'. But the whole site – 'there are really three castles connected with each other by three drawbridges' – was in such a dilapidated state and the grounds so unkempt and overgrown with weeds, that only their knowledge of the history enacted there could invest it with interest.

Then on Sunday morning they 'shaped for Paris', finding their journey very tedious, partly perhaps because they were a little weary. As George said in his diary:

'This travelling and sight-seeing business is hard work.'

At least, through John Keppie's good offices (he had spent a year at the École des Beaux Arts in Paris), they had a hotel to go to – Madame Pirie's Hôtel Britannique behind the Opera – which was comfortable and moderate, considering the high prices being paid in Paris at that time. For this was 1889, the year of the great Universal Exhibition, which was far in advance of its predecessors in glamour and size and scope *and* it had the Eiffel Tower as its main attraction.

They went out to supper at Lissauts in the Palais Royal, though George could not manage anything ('something has gone wrong with the works'), but he did think: 'of how often Father must have done the same thing on this very Sunday more than twenty years ago in this same place!' They adjourned to the Café de la Paix, all of them agreeing that they would prefer a quieter evening than battling their way through the crowds would give them. Even so, it was after midnight when they got back to their hotel, having been fascinated by the endless stream of people of all nationalities strolling past.

George stayed in on the Monday morning but in the afternoon sallied out with his friends to the Exhibition site on the Champs de Mars. They looked at the paintings first but there were so many rooms that 'we hurried through some of the minor schools'. At least on Monday George could do justice to his dinner. Then they wandered over the grounds, 'all beautifully illuminated with electric, Chinese and other lamps – and only managed to explore about a quarter of the place.' As one who had been closely involved with the Glasgow Exhibition, George remarked ruefully:

'There are incredible numbers being admitted to the Exposition every day – as many in a day in fact as we got in a good week in the Glasgow Exhibition.'

The Eiffel Tower met with their considered approval:

'We had heard and read so much about its being a foolish undertaking and a blot on a beautiful city that we were pleased to find . . . it a graceful structure . . . the construction a perfect marvel of lightness.' The Exposition site included the Trocadero by a special bridge built over the river, but its former glamour, as George remembered it, 'was quite dimmed by the dazzle of the present show.' By the end of the day, George was exhausted and slept 'like a top'.

In the morning (Tuesday 27 August), they paid their respects to Notre Dame, visited the Morgue and 'shaped for the Exposition again'. They spent the whole of the rest of the day there: went up the Eiffel Tower; inspected Eddison's Phonograph; admired the grand proportions and simple construction of the 'Galerie des Machines'; wandered through the 'street in Cairo and some of the representative architecture of the different countries, which struck us as being true models', and finally left at nine o'clock, adjourning to a café in the Boulevard des Capucines and watching the world go by.

Wednesday 28 August was their last day together. They spent it: 'running all over the place and enjoying ourselves. We were in the Louvre, the Musée de Cluny, through the new Sorbonne and saw a very fine fresco by Paul Baudry . . . '

The next day John Keppie and the others started back home and George went eastward, 'feeling all right again,' he wrote, 'but I won't be sorry to get a bracing from the fine Swiss Mountain air.'

He was a good traveller. His own keen interest in everybody and everything evoked a generous response. The long, hot journey to Lucerne, starting from Paris at 7.30 a.m. and not arriving till eleven at night, passed pleasantly because he had the company of some English tourists who knew the route. He went for a sail up Lake Lucerne next morning, the boat reminding him of: 'our pet river boat at home, the *Ivanhoe*.'

When he was sketching in the afternoon he was surprised to be approached by 'a young American lady, who spoke to me without any reserve and asked me to do the drawing for her sketch'. Looking back afterwards, he found he had enjoyed the encounter.

He went on by the great St Gotthard Railway, full of admiration for it as a 'magnificent piece of engineering'. Again, 'I was most fortunate to have had for a fellow traveller a most intelligent gentleman who seemed to know every inch of the road.' The next day at Como, 'not much of a place', he was almost blasted out of his bed at a very early hour, by the band accompanying the locals on their day's outing, playing under his window. 'The Italians are a *very noisy* people,' he remarked, 'and it takes a good deal of sound to please their bandmasters.'

Milan, his next port of call, was a disappointment: the Bréra had a very fine collection of paintings and sculpture but the Cathedral compared very unfavourably with those he had seen in France and even Leonardo's 'Last Supper' did not move him as much as he had expected. So he did not linger in what he termed 'a Glasgow in Italy'.

His reaction to the Certosa at Pavia was very different: 'The façade as a whole and its parts in detail, are so beautiful in design and execution that this building might well be called "The Poem" . . . the effect of light and shade in the loggia was finer than anything I have yet seen.'

The architect in him responded to many of the buildings in Verona: 'It was perhaps the most useful town in that respect that I have yet visited,' but there and in Padua, 'every second man you meet is a lazy officer, who spends his whole day, swaggering up and down and sipping coffee at a café.'

His most spontaneous raptures were reserved for Venice, where he arrived on Friday 6 September:

'I have been in a sort of happy dreamland since. Oh lovely Venice! More lovely and fascinating than my wildest dreams have ever suggested to me.' The approach by train, 'where we saw Venice gradually growing into itself. The station, 'quiet and orderly,' a marked contrast to 'the boisterous din and row' of other Italian railway stations. 'In five minutes, I was comfortably seated in a gondola and was gliding along noiselessly to my hotel. The gondolier began to sing and I really thought I must be in dreamland . . . ' Over dinner he discovered congenial company in two of his fellow guests: How, an American and Lagergnen, a Swede, 'a very clever fellow', speaking seven or eight languages very fluently and very knowledgeable about Venice, past and present.

All three then took a gondola, 'moving about as if it were a lovely black swan', and went down the Grand Canal, listening to the music carrying over the water: 'I cannot describe what I felt like but I know I was too much enraptured to utter a single word.' Back at the hotel, 'I went to bed and dreamt and tried to imagine the mosquitos were not eating me up.'

Saturday morning found him in St Mark's, 'once more struck dumb.' He thought the cathedral: 'beautiful in design, proportion and effect and quite unique, in perfect keeping with everything else in this truly unique place.' He had read his Ruskin and did not always agree with his pronouncements:

'How absurd even great men are sometimes!'

To his great content, 'after dinner, I was once more invited to spend the evening with my friends and, if possible, I enjoyed it more than my first evening.' He was determined not to miss any opportunities and indeed the many places he mentions show how well he had prepared himself, from the Tintorettos in the Scuola di San Rocco, to the Academia, to the great church of San Francisco where he saw the monuments to Titian and Canova. On the last morning in Venice he tried wandering through the narrower streets but found it a bewildering and unsavoury experience. It did not diminish, however, his rapturous memories of his experience of Venice.

On his way to Florence he called in at Bologna and would have liked to stay longer but he knew all that lay before him still and pressed on. Florence did not disappoint him but he found: 'it is no easy work going through these large picture galleries but they are full of such gems that one never thinks of fatigue,' – or very rarely. One afternoon he retreated to the Boboli Gardens, after having kept hard at it in the Uffizi and only managed half of what he had intended, 'though I think I have impressed some (of the pictures) permanently on my memory.'

At the end of another day in Florence he wrote:

'Tonight I am very tired – am thinking of turning in soon so as to be fit for another good day's work tomorrow.' Not the reaction of a dilettante. He spent a day or two longer than he had intended there because the money he was expecting had not arrived and he had to wait for it. But of all that he saw in Florence, and it was a formidable tally, what stirred his imagination most was the monastery of San Marco: 'I felt like an old brother walking through the cells, all so beautifully frescoed . . . to me Fra Angelico's work here is as near perfection as it is possible to come.'

Rome was his next goal, but he decided to break his journey at Siena and was so enchanted with it that he couldn't resist staying overnight there. He came across: 'a young American fellow who is here studying architecture and who, when he knew what I was doing, very kindly consented to show me round the town. Have I not been most fortunate in my friends since parting with my chums at Paris?' (It might be his daughters, Winifred and Alison, speaking.)

In Rome he pursued his architectural interests as seriously as ever. He was somewhat daunted by the sheer distance between the places he wanted to see, 'and every place of interest is on such a grand scale.' But he did valiantly, making a serious attempt to decide why he was disappointed in St Peter's. He even went right to the top of the great dome, having obtained special permission from the sacristan, and:

'I must say it is a wonderful piece of construction but even here I was not satisfied. I'm afraid I went to see an ideal – and am glad I did not see it.' And he goes on with a description of all the things he did admire or was interested in.

He was six nights and seven days in Rome (18 to 25 September). By Monday (he had arrived the previous Wednesday), 'I was dead beat and had to stay in the house and spent an enjoyable, quiet evening with our genial host.' He had had to move from his first place because it was too expensive; his genial host was in the more modest pensione.

He left Rome on Wednesday (25th), travelling overnight to Naples to save time – and there the diary ends. Rome had rather defeated him as a diarist: the Pantheon, the Vatican, the Forum, the view from the Pincian Hill, all evoked a positive response. But so much of what he saw was already known to him through photographs and his studies and what was the point, he felt, of making: 'a few casual remarks about the principal places I visit?'

Those who have spent hectic days trying to 'see Rome' will feel some sympathy with him. Certainly, through the diary, we have got to know his zest for life, his enthusiastic, outgoing character, his dedication to his chosen profession, his straightforward, sensible approach, his essential trustworthiness.

He would have returned to Glasgow at the end of September. No doubt over the previous two months his 'Indian letters' would have been duly dispatched every week: one coming the other way was to change his life completely and draw a line under his hopes of making his way in the world as an architect, a profession for which he had prepared himself so well.

George with his Fiat in Bombay

When Winifred and Alison were shown this photograph by their mother, they roared with laughter at the old fashioned car. But their mother indignantly told them that it had been an expensive up-to-date Fiat in white and red. On the occasion of George V's coronation durbar in Bombay, George and Mary McKenzie were the unwitting outriders of the royal party in this car, preceding the King and Queen and cheered by the crowds.

3

Life in Bombay, 1889–96

Sometime in the last three months of 1889, George heard from his father that he must return to Bombay and take over the running of the business. No question of choice: it was something he must do. The reason for this was that his father, when out sailing, had suddenly felt blindness strike one of his eyes. Glaucoma was diagnosed and, in something of a panic, he demanded that his eldest son should take his place in the business of supervising the workforce in the sawmills.

For the sake of his parents and his younger brothers and sisters, George had to go – and for seven years he bore the main responsibility for the running of the mills, before being joined by any of his brothers. It *was* a sacrifice: one which probably his family were unaware of or chose to ignore. Alexander McKenzie wanted to show his equal regard for all his sons but equality of sacrifice was not demanded of the younger ones: Harry became an eye specialist; Charles went into the Indian Forestry Commission; Alex, in the end, established his own woollen factory in Scotland and lived in Helensburgh; it was Ken who joined the business and, when George died, reaped the profit of all his hard work, because a big expansion of railway building greatly increased demand, which led to greater profits from the sawmills.

Not that George repined. He knew after all, what to expect of conditions of life in Bombay, such as the general prevalence of dirt in most of the city; health hazards from polluted water, plague-carrying rats, smallpox and so on. He knew he would have to put up with prickly heat in the oppressive humidity of summer. He knew he would find few to share his interests in the arts and architecture and that social life in Bombay would too often be oppressively formal. On the question of relations with his Indian servants and staff, he had no worries: they were ready to serve him devotedly. It helped that he knew Hindi and they realized that they had a good master. Their desire to please him meant that they would try to tell him what they thought he wanted to hear, however often he demanded to be told the truth.

Among the staff alone, thirteen different religions were practised, with a complicated range of ritual observances, but they all went their own ways peacefully. They did not take kindly to ideas of western medicine. George wanted to get all his workmen vaccinated when there was a severe outbreak of smallpox. He knew there would be resistance because smallpox was regarded in some way as a blessing from the gods, so he assembled his workforce and before them all was inoculated himself. Then he turned to his personal servant who stepped up to do his duty: as the skin was scratched and the vaccine rubbed on he fainted dramatically – and George had to begin all over again.

He proved more than equal to the managerial job that had been thrust upon him and he became director of a number of other local companies, which meant he was well enough off to return to Scotland every two years or so and that kept him in touch with friends made there and with what he had learnt to value in his experience of Europe. For instance he decided he was tired of the various reds of the ordinary durries (rugs) – he wanted something cooler to the eye – so, remembering the tiles he had seen and sketched in one of the châteaux of the Loire, he designed rugs in white and two shades of blue, had them specially made, and spread them on the floors throughout the bungalow.

He had the opportunity in Bombay to indulge his passion for horses: he could do anything with a horse. His own stables, where the carriages were kept, were at the foot of the garden and he may even, Winifred thinks, have owned a race horse. Certainly he was a member of the West India Turf Club and never missed a race meeting if he could help it. He also joined the Bombay Light Horse and was on duty with them during the plague riots, Bombay being devastated by outbreaks of bubonic plague in the years following

1897. He had to go to identify his coachman, who had died in the plague hospital, and the doctor there said grimly to him that there were enough rats in his stables alone to spread plague all over Bombay.

He also welcomed the motor car with enthusiasm and bought a stylish, white Fiat, lined with red, to drive in Bombay. Later, after his marriage to Mary, in 1911 when King George V and Queen Mary were in Bombay for their coronation durbar, his Fiat was the last vehicle to go down the main street before the royal procession. It tickled his sense of humour to drive beneath banners proclaiming 'Welcome George and Mary', and that he and *his* Mary should receive the first cheers as they, unintentionally acting as outriders, drove in their Fiat between the assembled crowds.

Like his father before him, he became a Free Mason, a member of Lodge Truth, and for a time a Grand Lodge officer. He was also a keen bridge player and took up golf with enthusiasm, though he used to get up at five in the morning in order to fit in a game and escape the worst heat of the day. Then he would come in, hastily eat a banana and be off to work. There is no doubt that with all his zest for life and readiness to fit in all he could, he had to work hard. In one of his letters home he wrote:

'We are working from eight in the morning to nine-thirty in the evening.'

But he had also worked out this pattern of life which included worthwhile visits home to Scotland and by 1896, when he was thirty, decided that it was high time he was married.

The Little Mem-sahib

Winifred in full command, out walking with her ayah and boy.

George with his Family

In the garden at Ravenswood: Winifred, Alison, George, Mary and Alec. Mary McKenzie divided her time between Bombay with her husband and Bridge of Weir with her children.

4

Marriage, 1896–1913

George's choice of a wife was Jessie, sister of his friend Bob Wallace. They were married in 1896, and, on 13 January 1897, Alec, George's only son, was born in Bombay. About two years later, Jessie succumbed to one of Bombay's killer diseases and George was left a widower. With him being so much at work, Alec was taken into the care of his grandparents.

George still continued his visits to Scotland and in 1903 he was over with his younger brother, Ken. Ken was engaged to marry Amy Osborne, a younger daughter of James Osborne of Thornton Hall. Her eldest sister, Mary, the most enterprising and resourceful of her large family and a gifted violinist, was planning to go to Germany for further training. She had already spent a year at school in Vevey, in Switzerland, where she had gained a good knowledge of French.

George was invited with his brother to Thornton Hall to meet his future sister-in-law, Amy, and was at once much struck by Mary. Her mother, half way through dinner, said:

'You must excuse Mary and Margaret: they are going in to Glasgow for a concert they very much want to hear.' (Margaret was the second sister of Mary and a good pianist.)

George, resolute not to miss this opportunity, suddenly 'recollected' a pressing matter of business that he really had to see his brother-in-law about in Glasgow. It wasn't a very good excuse but it served its immediate purpose though it left Amy feeling aggrieved. Within a week George and Mary were engaged. That was in May. By October they were married (much to Amy's chagrin: she definitely felt that her elder sister had stolen a march on her).

This was a love match without doubt and George, remembering what an enchantment Venice had cast upon him, was determined to take Mary there. They had to go back to India but a leisurely journey was planned with Venice as its highlight. Winifred recollects her mother telling her how George would exuberantly rival the gondolier in calling out warnings as they came to corners on the canals. Mary did not take kindly to 'continental breakfasts' and felt aggrieved when she saw a plate of fish emerging from the kitchen, only to find it was put down in triumph before her, George having plotted with the chef to arrange this.

When they arrived in Bombay they were garlanded with flowers and Mary remembered standing in the hot sun during the speech of welcome, delivered in Hindi. She, of course, didn't understand a word but was given a very real insight into George's relations with his staff when she glanced at him during the speech and saw tears streaming down his face, so moved was he at the devotion which lay behind the words.

They had to stay in the family house at first – George after all had not been planning to bring back a bride – and the next challenge for Mary was getting on to good terms with her stepson. Alec had been at prep school in the hills and when he came home, (he was only seven) he blurted out:

'The boys say that step-mothers are cruel!'

So Mary said:

'Well Alec! Some are, and some aren't.'

Since he soon realized she was in the latter category, all was well and remained well even after the death of his father.

The three of them then moved to 'Mount Ida', their bungalow on Cumbala Hill, and Mary adjusted herself to a new pattern of life. It was very formal. Etiquette decreed with whom she had to leave cards in Bombay society. Those who received cards from her had to return her calls. She had a box with 'Not at Home' on it and a slit in the top for cards (Winifred remembers playing with it when she was small). Callers would, she hoped, just drop their cards into this box, even though they could hear the mistress of the house practising the violin. For Mary kept up her music. Notices survive of her playing in concerts in Bombay: in 1908 for the YMCA, and later in 1912 in the Royal Opera House in a charity concert with an impressive turn-out of all the Bombay bigwigs.

There had been a large staff at Thornton Hall. In Bombay it was more like an army. On one occasion she feared a riot had broken out with shouted commands and counter-commands and a mêlée of struggling bodies. It proved to be the arrival of her father-in-law's gift to her of a piano – and it was in the end brought safely into the bungalow. It was a strange and very isolated life for her in many ways. Her husband went off to work early and she was left with this army of servants. If she went out at all, it had to be in her carriage, and as the only two words she could manage at first were 'Go' and 'Return', she did not feel very secure.

As a bride she was invited to many dinners, and etiquette decreed that all the guests should take their special servants with them to stand behind their chairs at dinner (to be sure they were served with what they liked). Dinner tables were always elaborately set, with decorations down the centre and a formidable muster of glasses at each place. Winifred remembers her mother showing her a set of the finest lawn mats exquisitely embroidered with a bramble pattern. These mats were put on the fruit plates of each guest and on them a finger bowl with scented water or perhaps a flower in the water. Etiquette decreed that when it came to the fruit course, the bowl should be put on the mat. One nervous bachelor moved his bowl but forgot the mat and spooned his ginger in syrup on to it.

Evening dress consisted of a long skirt and a long-sleeved bodice with a low-cut neckline. Coming in one evening, Mary took her bodice off and threw it over the back of a chair. Picking it up the next morning, it felt very heavy – and a musk rat fell out.

It was the heat which troubled her most: it was inescapable in those days and she often found herself crying with it. Then there were the ants and the ubiquitous mosquitos, which meant always sleeping under nets. To frustrate the ants, the furniture was stood in water; to frustrate the mosquitos from breeding in the water, special insecticide had to be put in. It was a complicated life!

Then, on 23 August 1905, a daughter, Winifred, was born to them. Mary's mother, Mrs Osborne, had come out to Bombay to help her daughter and welcome her first grandchild. Unhappily she caught cholera – at the time the only case in Bombay – and died within two days, in her daughter's bungalow, just six weeks before Winifred was born. Her great friend, Mrs Liston, the wife of the head of the medical department in Bombay, and herself a nurse, would not let Mary go near her mother and insisted on nursing Mrs Osborne, although she too was pregnant.

When Winifred was about a year old, the family returned to Scotland and she had her first journey through the Red Sea. They had had their alarms before this happened. The sofa on their 'Mount Ida' verandah should have been moved away from the rail round it – her mother and father knew by now, as Winifred aged little more than one, had said, 'Baba *must* climb' – but this had not been done. The child came running out on to the verandah, jumped on to the sofa when she saw her doll there and went head first over the rail. Mary picked her up and saw, to her horror, a triangular hole in Winifred's forehead. She summoned her husband and the doctor, prevented the ayah from bathing the wound with unsterilized water and, when help arrived, held Winifred until the edges of the wound had been drawn together and stitched – so that all that remains is a neat scar on the left temple.

On the voyage home, she took an ayah to help with Winifred. With Bombay receding fast into the distance, the ayah came rushing up on deck, shouting:

'Tell Captain Sahib to stop the ship! Forgotten brush for baby's bottle!'

The two of them had their work cut out to keep an eye on the child, who was running about, all over the ship. Back home, Mary's sisters agreed she was a nonpareil but were scornful of George's earlier description of the colour of her eyes:

'Violet! What nonsense! They're *brown.*'

George and Mary's second daughter, Alison, was born, also in

Bombay, on 30 August 1907, and it wasn't only George who was thrilled then. Winifred, aged two, who had no idea of what had been happening, ran in to see her mother. To her astonishment, she saw this tiny baby as well, so out she rushed, shouting:

'Nan, Nan! Boy, boy! Chota (small) baba in there!'

When all was explained to her, it was even more satisfactory for 'the thrill I had with my sister then lasted all our lives'.

George had been returning regularly to Scotland before he was married and would rent a house for the months of his stay. Now, with a family, he began to plan for a permanent home in Scotland with thoughts of retiring from India and taking up work in Glasgow. Probably in 1909, he bought a villa in Bridge of Weir called 'Ravenswood', his choice being determined by his friends, the Farquhars, owning the house next door. The whole family came back together to settle in, with an ayah to look after Alison. The ayah had not encountered gaslight before and when George and Mary were going out one evening, they impressed upon her that she should not touch the gas. She didn't touch it but she blew it out, and when the parents returned they found the house full of fumes.

It was time for Alec to be going to secondary school so he was launched at Merchiston Castle, and when Alison emerged from babyhood, a governess, Miss Hain, was engaged to take responsibility for the girls. Mary divided her time between her husband in Bombay and her children. Winifred remembers almost nothing about the inside of 'Ravenswood' – the garden meant everything, especially with the Farquhar children next door. There was a revolving summer house and a lawn for games. There were boxwood hedges round the vegetable garden and beyond that a stream going through a little wood where the children would play and Miss Hain would sit sketching.

Looking back, Winifred thinks she can trace some formative influences on their development as artists to this golden time. Their father, for instance, in a letter to his little daughter, Winifred, in February 1911, ended with:

'You must ask your Mother to give you [aged six] a paint box and one for Alison [aged four] too and they are from me . . . '

And they were lucky in Miss Hain, who interested them in her sketching and painting.

Winifred's sense of colour, in design especially, was fostered by her early interest in collecting stamps. Her father sent her some in every weekly letter and on her birthday in 1911 she received a three-cornered Cape of Good Hope stamp. Before she could read she could recognize which countries the stamps came from by their designs and would come running to her mother to tell her of one from Australia, or wherever, which she had identified by the design.

The years at Ravenswood were a happy time for the girls, especially the month of August, which they shared, as regards birthdays, with the three Farquhar children next door – so that there seemed to be a party every week. At Christmas too there were some memorable parties. George, writing to Winifred on 23 January 1913, commented:

'What fun you had being inside that plum pudding. I wish I had been there to see you.'

She does in fact remember distributing the presents after emerging as the plum pudding fairy. This was only two months before his death. Only a little earlier, he had also written:

'I have so much work to do, I have no time to get ill.'

There was a sad irony in that because in March of 1913 the blow fell. Since the post took three weeks between Scotland and India, Mary and George had worked out a telegraphic code for emergencies, and through it came an urgent message that George was very ill with enteric fever. Mary set off at once, didn't notice that the train was going east and not south and was bewildered to find herself at the Forth Bridge. This didn't prevent her boarding the ship she had been aiming at, but by the time it reached Egypt, news came through Cairo that George had died. Would she like to go back?

She decided to go on.

She didn't know a soul on board and felt she had to speak to someone. She chose a couple whose faces looked kind; they were doctors and they befriended her till she reached Bombay.

The funeral was over, of course, before she arrived. But at least George's brother, Ken, was there and was able to tell her in what high regard and affection George had been held and how devoted his workmen were. His personal servant even broke caste to help carry George's coffin.

George's sudden death at the age of only forty-seven meant a great change in the pattern of life for his wife and children but the *quality* of their lives had been moulded by him: by his love for his family; by the wide horizons of his imagination; by his relish of the opportunities for enjoyment that came his way; by his acceptance of responsibility and readiness to work hard. All these qualities can be seen in the way his wife and children lived their lives after his death.

Mary McKenzie with her Daughters

This photograph was taken to send to George in Bombay, to show off his present of beaver furs to them.

Silhouette of Mary McKenzie with her Violin

Mary had always wanted to play the violin but had promised her father that, up to the age of ten, she would learn the piano only. Her father kept his side of the promise and on her tenth birthday he gave her her first violin. Her aunts disapproved; they thought it very unsuitable for a woman. (This was echoed by the nurse in Bombay after Winifred was born, who said in triumph: "That will be the end of your violin now!") When she was twenty-one her father gave her a really good violin, which she continued to play all her life.

5

Kilmacolm, 1913–23

'Ravenswood' had to go, following the death of George McKenzie and Mary McKenzie was left, a widow after only ten years of marriage, with a stepson and two young daughters and a much diminished income. Under her husband's will, a trust had been set up to provide for the family. Only some money George had invested in a firm in Scotland (with a view to his retirement from India) yielded sizable dividends and, not being subject to the terms of the trust, later provided a source of capital when it was needed.

Mrs McKenzie now inevitably took centre stage. *She* had to take the difficult decisions; had to balance the family finances; had to embody authority both for her stepson and her daughters; had to set the horizons, in circumstances in which she found herself very much alone. As an Osborne, she had been closest both intellectually and in spirit to her father. But he had died and the rest of the family lacked the imagination to put themselves in her place; they just went their own ways. At Christmas, for instance – the one following George's death – two of her sisters took themselves off to Bombay to visit friends: it never occurred to them that this would bring home to their sister her loneliness and the sense of responsibilities weighing upon her. In one direction at any rate she had no worries: Winifred and Alison were endlessly happy in each other's company, and never bored. Alec liked to argue – it was part of his process of growing up – but he always regarded her as his mother and was never estranged from her or from his sisters and knew that their home was his.

The house which she bought in what was called the 'wrong end' of Kilmacolm, was a new, semi-detached villa, which seemed small to the family after Bridge of Weir. She called the house

'Mount Ida' after her Bombay home; she and the girls shared the big bedroom, Alec had the next, which meant there was a spare room for guests. A cook could be afforded – there was a small room off the kitchen for her – and although the succession of cooks often complicated life (one of them proved to have a taste for red biddy) – they did lighten the load for her.

She then had to decide about education: Alec was sent to Glasgow Academy, because of financial stringency, and Winifred started at St Columba's in Kilmacolm. Alison was too young for school but her mother found a young Scottish girl, Miss Cant, who had never taught before at all: she was persuaded to take charge of Alison's first steps in learning and she proved most successful and went from strength to strength later with other families. After two years, Alison joined Winifred at St Columba's and the two of them used to walk through the village to school, stopping on the way at the grocer's shop. In front of the counter – there were six biscuit jars with glass tops, and every morning weighty decisions had to be taken about which biscuits to buy with their tuppences. The shop assistants were endlessly patient and the satisfied sisters would trot out of the shop with their little pokes containing their mid-morning snacks.

The other shop in the village which the sisters enjoyed was the draper's. There they would ask to see the boxes of cotton reels and would gloat over the colours and choose the ones which most took their fancy, though at this stage they never thought the cottons might be used for sewing. This was when they had sufficient in their 'bank account' – for their mother acted as their banker, giving them receipts for any money they might have been given for birthday presents and never questioning their right to withdraw what they wanted from her 'bank box'. After their mother died they found a scrap of paper she had kept, being a note that they had 'taken out five shillings', all duly signed in their childish handwriting.

There was no anxiety in those days about traffic: in fact the girls used to practise slow bicycle rides along what is now the main Port Glasgow road. They would also hang over the garden gate to watch the great Clydesdales and other horses going to the fairs with their brasses shining and their tails plaited with ribbons. Then they would watch for their return from the judging, to see who were the winners – often disapproving of the judges' choices. Beyond the back-garden fence at 'Mount Ida', there was country to be explored with corncrakes and buntings in the fields and a wealth of wild flowers both there and in the marsh and wood beyond. But Alison was terrified that the frequent notices saying 'Trespassers will be prosecuted' meant that, if an angry farmer found them (once one had from a distance shaken a stick at them), he would cut off their heads!

Like their father they felt the cold and damp in winter and suffered badly from chilblains. Sometimes on their way to school when they felt the cold making their fingers and toes ache, they tried imagining that they were on a journey through the desert, parched with heat and thirst and forcing themselves to struggle on to the hoped-for oasis, represented by the next lamp post.

In Winifred's memories of St Columba's, it is the gymnasium that comes to mind. There, once a day, all pupils had to put square wooden blocks on their heads and walk round, straight-backed, to improve deportment (to the accompaniment of the clatter of falling blocks). There too, lunch was taken, leaving behind it the smell of cabbage, etc; and there art lessons took place. Art was not held in much esteem in the school so, at each lesson everything had to be dug out, arranged and put away at the end; but even so Winifred loved those lessons.

The rest of school she enjoyed, especially following in the wake of her best friend, Elizabeth Handasyde, later to get a Double First at Cambridge. She would embark on courses on Greek and trigonometry and carry Winifred along in her wake, though precious little of what she learnt with Elizabeth stuck in her mind. Winifred also achieved a certain status in school, being put on 'the Franchise', which meant you were given a half day off occasionally. Alison, for some baffling reason, never got beyond 'recommended for the Franchise'.

In 1914 the First World War began. Alec, just eighteen years old, went straight into the army from Glasgow Academy. In 1915 he was given a commission as second lieutenant in the Royal Scots Fusiliers, in charge of forty-year-old tough regular soldiers, and sent out to France. 'I'm too young,' he would write despairingly to his mother. 'I'm too *young*.' In July of 1916, he was wounded – nine bullets in his lungs and spine – and sent to a hospital in Leicester, where his mother and Winifred visited him and where he slowly recovered.

The first impact of the war on Kilmacolm itself was with the arrival of refugees from the German invasion of Belgium in 1914. They were settled in some of the new houses near enough to the McKenzies for the girls to enjoy playing with the children of these Belgian families and for their mother to be involved because of her command of French. Through her music too she helped the local Belgian Relief Fund by playing in concerts, both as a soloist and with M. Jean Beghon, who had been conductor of one of the principal orchestras of Antwerp, and was pianist, singer and composer. Quite apart from public performances, Mrs McKenzie and her sister Margaret Osborne, a pianist, enjoyed playing together of an evening at 'Mount Ida', so the children, listening in the bedroom above, became familiar with a great deal of classical music.

Winifred also felt compelled, through appeals to her patriotism, to give up her much loved stamp album, for the 'war effort'. That was a wrench. She also remembers Armistice Day and the wave of excitement which swept through their community, with Union Jacks everywhere and 'loyal ribbons' in red, white and blue tied to the tails of cats and dogs.

Mrs McKenzie took another courageous and unselfish decision. She knew her husband had wanted their daughters to go to a public school and the fees could be met from the money which had accumulated from the dividends of the Scottish firm, which had been outside the terms of the trust. One of her brothers-in-law said to her: 'You can have lots of new dresses and pretty things with this,' but she was determined to send her daughters away to school to broaden their horizons and give them confidence.

She chose Priorsfield, near Godalming in Surrey, on the rec-
ommendation of Betty Farquhar, their neighbour from Bridge
of Weir. The school had been founded by Mrs Burton Brown
and Mrs Leonard Huxley, with Arnold's Rugby as a model.
Mrs Huxley had died, but her sons, Aldous and Julian, would
often come to Priorsfield to visit Mrs Burton Brown and her
daughter Bice. It was a school of about a hundred girls, all aged
between fourteen and eighteen. Many distinguished people and
those from the professional classes sent their daughters there and
some had their sons at Charterhouse nearby. They were divided
into forms and each form, among other activities, was expected to
produce a play, down to the last detail of scenery and programmes,
which fostered great 'esprit de corps' among the girls. They lived
together in the same house, which was surrounded by a fine garden.
The two McKenzies found the warmer weather a great source of
comfort and spent all the time they could outside, doing their prep
or playing tennis.

At Priorsfield, Winifred made a life-long friend, Eva Lawrie,
whom oddly enough she had seen on holiday at Gullane in East
Lothian, but never met there. Now they became firm friends,
brought together by their interest in, among other things, drawing
and wild flowers. As prefects they could be independent in their
walks, so out they went, armed with a Bentham and Hooker, to
find wild flowers and, without picking them, to identify them and
note the details and the location. It was a labour of love but they
also won a school prize for their collection.

The Headmistress was a Classics enthusiast who loved Greece
and Italy and opened the world of Greek and Italian art to the
Priorsfield girls through her own enthusiasm and through visits
to the major galleries and museums in London. Her own lectures
were an inspiration, supplemented by excellent outside speakers on
a great variety of subjects.

Art was taught by someone from the Slade, whom Winifred was
ready enough to follow, for she knew by this time that this was
her metier. She wanted to be an artist and Priorsfield confirmed
her in her ambition. But Alison's originality could not be slotted

in to Slade conventions and the art teacher seems to have made little effort to appreciate her gifts. The headmistress, on the other hand, thought highly of her intelligence and wanted her to try for Oxford. So what with being pulled towards an area of study she did not want and pushed away from one she did, Alison's last two years at Priorsfield were not happy. When she left, she said rather desperately to Winifred:

'Well! I'm going to try one year at the Glasgow School of Art, and if I'm no good I'll just take a course in domestic science.'

When it came to pursuing the careers of their choice, their mother gave her daughters her unfailing support: she unhesitatingly ruled the roost on every other subject, but not on that. The family was less understanding and quite unrestrained in expressing their amazement at Winifred's and Alison's choice of a career. One cousin ended an argument by exclaiming impatiently, 'Well! If you must go to art school for heaven's sake don't dress like artists!' while an aunt, with unconcealed scorn, voiced her surprise that boys wasted their time learning art – girls possibly, she conceded, though even here she couldn't really see the point. Winifred and Alison could, however: their compasses were set all right: henceforth, only the needs of others would *ever* divert them from their 'true north'.

6

Glasgow School of Art, 1923–30

Winifred enrolled at the Glasgow School of Art in 1923 and felt exhilarated at this new stage in her life. Going in by train on her own to Glasgow was something to be savoured. It made her feel she was out in the world. She looked forward eagerly to the prospect of spending the whole day on her art, among like-minded young people. It would be a testing of her vocation. Of course she still lived at home but it was only half an hour by train to St Enoch's station and though her mother insisted she should not stay late, which meant she could not join in any of the students' evening activities, she did not feel deprived or aggrieved. In those days it was the custom for the men and women students to be taught quite separately: it was only afterwards when she realized that Mackintosh Patrick and Ian Fleming and others, when she met them at later exhibitions, had been her contemporaries at the School, that the separate teaching seemed an odd convention.

The Glasgow School of Art's premises had been transformed since her father's day. A limited competition had been held in 1894 for plans for a new building for the School, and to Fra Newbery's delight, the one entered by Charles Rennie Mackintosh was accepted. It was a revolutionary design with its great windows and vertical lines and meticulous planning of the interior. It was not completed till 1909 but it proved to be a landmark in the history of twentieth-century architecture.

Charles Rennie Mackintosh had expounded the theory that in his system, the air should always be fresh because it was always being washed in some way: so the windows were never to be opened or the delicate balance of the system would be upset. To students, this method of ventilation simply didn't work and there were constant complaints about it. Moreover, with Glasgow's smoke and its pea-soup fogs, the windows became covered with black grime which made the studios dark, but cleaning the windows was an expensive business and the School authorities had come to grudge having them done 'too often' – so the studios were *frequently* dark. Winifred remembers how sometimes, on very overcast days, the students in desperation would open the windows and let in the light. Another snag to those using the building was that the handsome chandeliers over the stairs tended to drop glass drips on to the students' heads and, from the women's point of view, they were but poorly provided for in the matter of cloakrooms. But to work in a building of such architectural acclaim was a matter of pride.

The train to Glasgow started at Kilmacolm so, as the weather got colder, the guards would push metal warming pans, filled with hot water, into each carriage – there were no corridors then – to thaw out frozen feet. At the same time, porters would run along the top of the train and poke a taper down through the roof to light the gas mantles.

The Diploma course at the School was officially spread over five years but most of the students completed it in four. Winifred opted for the drawing and painting side and, in her first year, she also did metal work, ceramics, clay modelling and colour woodcuts. The drawing classes did not provide the stimulation or the widening of horizons to which she had been looking forward: the students did most of their work by copying. They were confronted with grimy plaster casts and told to draw them. Once, when Winifred, after six weeks, feeling dissatisfied with what she had done, asked if she could start again, the master replied, 'Oh no! You haven't solved nearly all the problems,' but made no attempt to show her what the problems were or how she might be more successful in solving them.

One member of staff did fire her with enthusiasm and that was Chica Macnab, who introduced her to colour woodcuts. When Chica left to get married, Winifred carried on with increasing success. In fact, the very first work she ever exhibited was a colour woodcut – 'The Valley of the Dee, Kirkcudbright'. She sent it to the Glasgow Institute and derived enormous satisfaction from seeing it hanging in the McLellan Galleries, and even more when she saw a red spot stuck on the corner: someone had actually liked it enough to buy it! She started and would have loved to continue with wood engraving but was put off by the master being so often drunk. In general, looking back over her first year, Winifred's impression was that the members of staff might be maestros in their own lines but they did not take their actual teaching seriously enough and they didn't encourage students to look outside the little world of the School.

The greatest artistic experience for Winifred in her first year was going to the exhibition of Japanese prints in Glasgow. She had been introduced to the art of the Renaissance at Priorsfield. At the School of Art, she had accepted the concept of classical modelling and of central perspective with a fixed viewpoint. She knew nothing of the exciting developments in French art in the nineteenth century which had owed so much to the impact of Japanese art – and now, here before her in the McLellan Galleries, was the work of some of the great Japanese masters: Hokusai, Utamaro, Hiroshige . . . It was a revelation to her of what could be achieved by simplicity of design, by the use of new angles of vision and the appreciation of clear colours. It certainly helped to give direction to her ambition to develop a greater mastery in the art of the colour woodcut.

From her second year, Winifred remembers Alan Main's Life Drawing classes. He was an interesting teacher. One phrase of his certainly stuck in her mind: the desirability of 'synthetic vision'.

There were models, of course, for the Life Drawing classes: they were always needed and in Charles Rennie Mackintosh's entrance hall were two of his distinctive high-backed settles, one labelled 'Models' and the other 'Visitors'. On one occasion Winifred saw with some glee that her dignified and formidably ladylike mother, who had come to meet her at the School, was sitting on the Models' Settle. One of their models was a very vivacious Italian who used, strictly 'sub rosa', to tell the students' fortunes and complained bitterly to them that the School authorities wouldn't have her for 'the bare skin'. 'I'm paid more for the bare skin,' she would explain.

One of their male models came on to them from the University medical school with little red and blue spots all over his body where the lecturers had been pointing out the various features. He was a very thin man who would pose for about half an hour and then, at the rest period when everyone would stop work, he would put on his spectacles and tie – his 'off-duty' wear – and read the newspaper.

From Winifred's last two years at the School, Anning Bell's lectures stand out. Forrester Wilson had a fine colour sense, and this heightened her awareness of this aspect of painting, but in accordance with the conventions of the day, he would set very literary subjects, such as 'Grief' or 'Patience'. There was one enthusiastic lecturer who was showing them examples of different types of heads and, carried away by the profiles she was looking at, said:

'You can see there is a drop at the end of this nose which is not pure Mediterranean!'

The students roared their appreciation and the phrase stuck.

Maurice Greiffenhagen was still the head of painting. He had been appointed back in 1906 and came to Glasgow for short stints, keeping his main base in London. The students felt he had to be taken very seriously – certainly he was of one mind with them on that – and they tended to try to produce designs which were as near to his type of painting as they could. Since the best work that the students saw was that done by the staff on the edge of their work, those whom Greiffenhagen chose to favour with his drawings considered themselves privileged.

At the end of their fourth year, with Diplomas achieved, most of the students rejoiced that their course was over:

'We can put away our brushes!' They could now become art teachers and had no intention of producing any more of their own work unless they had to.

But Winifred wanted to be an artist and there were at any

rate two kindred spirits in her year: Freda Bone (Mrs Sprot), niece of Muirhead Bone, and Jean Irwin, who later worked in the Kelvingrove Art Gallery.

When Alison came back from school she took Winifred to task over her appearance – she was in grave danger of 'dressing like an artist'. She had been so absorbed in the new regime that she had put on the same red-knitted woollen costume day after day, not noticing it was beginning to sag. This, with her cloche hat – useful to tilt at the right angle if you didn't feel like talking to your neighbour – and a cardboard case for her paints kept together with a strap, seemed to her perfectly adequate for travelling to Glasgow. But even Alec had entered a mild protest: 'Have you only got that costume to wear?' and Alison was quite sure steps must be taken, and she took them.

For her part, Alison chose the Design and Textile Diploma, and from the start she flourished at college. She was recognized at once as an outstandingly original student. The Design school seems to have been more enterprising in challenging their students, and encouraging them to produce their best work in different fields in an individual way. Alison had a chance to be herself and became one of the leading figures in her year, often winning the accolade in the various exercises that the students were set. She was awarded the Newbery Medal, the highest award of the year. With it went £66 towards a journey to Italy, but she couldn't go alone and the family couldn't afford, at that stage, to go with her. So the £66 went to the runner-up and Alison had the honour of having won the Medal, which helped to build up her confidence in her own powers as an artist. (Winifred, after Alison's death, gave the Medal – a very handsome bronze plaque – to Fra Newbery's granddaughter.) Alison then began working on her 'Nursery Rhymes' and 'Alice' panels as well as designs for posters.

Their mother, remembering her own early visits to Paris and the excitement and pleasure they had given her, wanted to take her own daughters there. When she went to see her lawyer about funding such an expedition, she must have shown that she was feeling a little apprehensive – it was so long since she herself had done any travelling – for he looked at her solemnly and observed:

'You know, Mrs McKenzie, I've heard of people going to Paris *and* I've heard of people coming home again!'

But nothing seemed to go right at the beginning. When they arrived at the Gare du Nord, they were held up by an invalid in their carriage, so all the porters had been taken by the time they got their luggage out. There was only a drunk taxi man, so they decided to take a chance with him. The odds on their safe arrival got longer with every corner round which they accelerated, especially after their useful 'hold-all' fell on his driving foot and helped to increase the pace. The hotel proved to be behind the Opera, very much where their father had stayed as a student. But their mother was disappointed, especially when they went down to a meal and had to sit at a long table and put up their hands over whether they wanted 'soup, thick or clear?'. But she threw off her sense of discouragement and the three of them enjoyed themselves immensely. She even managed to get a box at the 'Opéra Comique' to see 'Carmen', for the same price as the seats she had originally asked for. Winifred also remembers a wonderful design exhibition they saw then.

Back in Kilmacolm, the family faced the fact that 'Mount Ida' simply wasn't big enough for them all now. Mother and daughters were still sharing one bedroom and Alec's was really too small for him. So the decision was made and the house was put up for sale. In their search for a bigger house in Kilmacolm, what clinched the family's choice of a square, stone-built villa, was the name engraved on the stone gate posts: 'Ravenswood', taking them back to their golden Bridge of Weir days.

Now for the first time, Winifred and Alison had a bedroom to themselves and took great pleasure in choosing their curtains and arranging their furniture. *AND* – crowning glory – they had a room upstairs as their studio, in which they could work and put up their easels with a sense of permanence. But Winifred's next year was not, in fact, spent in the studio but at Jordanhill Training College, doing a teacher's training course for which she had to live in digs in Glasgow. She got very little from the course. Quite a lot of it simply irritated her and what she found frustrating was being whisked from one school to another, and never having a chance to get to know a class well enough to do anything worthwhile with them. But she remembers an incident when the children had been asked to illustrate a man being chased by a bear. One little boy was finishing his drawing, head down on paper, and pencil going round and round and across and across in a black ball. When Winifred had prised up his head from his drawing, she saw a man up a tree with a bear at the foot of it and, away to the side, this black ball-thing. She asked what it was and the little chap was most indignant that she hadn't recognized that 'that was the *noise* the bear was making'.

A family wedding in Bath in 1930 gave the McKenzies a pointer towards their next move. Their cousin, May Pearson, was there and suggested that the girls should come to stay with her in Hampstead for three weeks and explore London. This splendid idea led to three exhilarating weeks which gave them the freedom of London. They loved it so much that their mother began to wonder if it would not be possible to move there. She herself loved London and she would enjoy being near her much-loved cousins, (the Pearsons); her daughters had completed their courses; Alec had a job as a chartered accountant with Cooper & Co in Glasgow and was now independent – so together they decided on London. In spite of the warnings of a neighbour, who kept telling them about the forty houses already on the market in Kilmacolm, 'Ravenswood' was put on the market and sold within two days. It was a clear confirmation of their decision and they could now go with light hearts on the holiday they had planned – their first visit to Italy.

Winifred's Priorsfield friend, Eva Lawrie, joined them. She was engaged to be married to Dr Maynard Gerrard, an Irishman. The wedding in St Giles was to be soon after their return from Italy and Winifred was to be one of the four bridesmaids. It was suggested to Eva that she might like to cry off the holiday but she was adamant that she wanted to go with them and was duly pursued by letters from her fiancé every day. The McClures, who had a flat on the Trinitá del Monte, overlooking the Spanish Steps, had booked rooms for them in a nearby hotel.

Like their father before them, the McKenzie sisters found Italy intoxicating. Just a brief walk up the Via Trinitá del Monte were the Borghese Gardens, where Winifred remembers especially the Judas trees in full bloom. The Forum, where they had expected from classroom prints to see only bleak piles of masonry, proved to be a delight, with wild flowers of all descriptions and trees in bloom on the Palatine. St Peter's, especially the interior, did weigh on the spirit, as it had on their father's. What added to this feeling was that it was Lent and all the altar crosses – and even Michelangelo's Pieta – were shrouded in purple.

They loved the journey through Tuscany to Siena, with the hilltop towns and the stripling Tiber and the abundance of flowers. Their response to Florence was whole-hearted: they could take it in in a way that was impossible in Rome. For Winifred, Donatello's enigmatic David, in the open gallery in the Bargello, brought home to her the full, authoritative impact of sculpture – a different matter altogether from the repugnance she had grown to feel for the dead-white plaster casts, grimed with Glasgow soot, of her School of Art days. But it was the monastery of San Marco, with Fra Angelico's frescoes, which most inspired their affection as well as admiration. Here again, though they did not know it then, their reaction was the same as their father's. Eva too shared all their enthusiasm, and the diary their mother kept shows how memorable this first visit was for them all. And they were in the Piazza del Duomo on Easter Day for the ceremony of the 'Scoppio del Carro', when they saw the white speck of the firework dove come shooting out of the west door before it whizzed back – amid cheers. It had flown well, which meant a good year for the Florentines.

To her chagrin, Winifred had to return to Glasgow for a term's teaching in Laurel Bank, having been engaged before the great London plan had been formulated. This meant that their mother and Alison went on ahead to look for a suitable base for their London adventure.

Alison's Free Photograph

These photographs of the sisters would never have baen taken if they had not seen a notice in the window of 'John Barnes' shop on the Finchley Road.

Winifred's Free Photograph

The window notice said: 'Buy two pairs of silk stockings and get a free photograph.'

7

London, 1930–40

Alison and her mother found, in their house-hunting, that it came down to a choice between a maisonette with service and a flat in a modern block which had just been finished. They chose the flat in the modern block – Alvanley Court. It was on the seventh floor and gave them magnificent views: to the south over London as far as the Crystal Palace (which they saw on fire in 1936) and to the north, up to Hampstead.

The choice of the flat meant that they would have to make some firm decisions about furniture. They looked at a family portrait of Auntie Black in its huge gilt frame: it was impossible to imagine it in their new London flat. There was simply nowhere for it to go, and, as it happened, she was a very plain-looking woman (though she must have been wealthy, since several portraits of her had been painted). The version the McKenzies had inherited had a further drawback. When James Osborne, Winifred's grandfather, was a little boy at Thornton Hall, he had shot a pea at the portrait and it had gone straight through Auntie Black's mouth (he was a very good shot). The hole had been patched up but did nothing to improve her looks so the McKenzies decided the best thing to do was to burn it, frame and all – so the portrait disappeared on a bonfire.

A few years later, Winifred and Alison were invited to a big lunch party given by the Edinburgh Pagans and the question of Auntie Black came up. Hadn't three portraits of Auntie Black been painted? What had happened to the third? Winifred and Alison, on opposite sides of the table, looked at each other, hoping their faces wouldn't give them away. They didn't, and the secret about her going up in smoke was safe for the time being. The other result of their choosing the flat was that they had to buckle to and learn how to cook, which later, when the war came, proved to have been a very useful lesson, Alison particularly taking pride in her cuisine.

But all this was secondary to their art: their London years were a time of real growth and exhilaration as their creative gifts as artists flowered. Chica Macnab had suggested to them that when they got to London they should try the Grosvenor School of Modern Art in Warwick Square. It had been started by her brother, Iain Macnab, in 1925 and for Winifred and Alison the advice proved to be invaluable, for it brought them into the orbit of one of the most outstanding teachers of his day, who was also an artist of wide achievement and of rare mastery in his chosen medium: wood engraving.

Iain Macnab was a Scot, born in the Philippines but brought up in Scotland, his family having settled, on their return home, in Kilmacolm. His parents had insisted that he should take a course in accountancy. He had no intention of making it his career but it did prove useful when, later on, he was organizing art societies and exhibitions. In 1914 he had joined the Highland Light Infantry, had had a shell explode near him at Loos but was rescued and somehow recovered, though he had to return to hospital often because of those war injuries. He had then taken himself to the Glasgow School of Art and from there to London and then Paris. Now, at the Grosvenor School, through his generosity of mind, his skill as a teacher, his friendships with other artists, he naturally attracted serious students, all of them post-graduates, who went on to do good work in all fields of art – but especially in print making, in which he himself had achieved superb effects of classical harmony. But the Grosvenor School was not alone in concentrating on wood engraving: it was a feature of art all over Europe in the twenties and thirties.

For Winifred and Alison, this was a time of hard but creative work in learning new disciplines. Iain Macnab would suggest a subject and set a limited time in which to produce a design for it, a design which had to be contained within a definite frame.

Then, about once a month, he would bring in artists, who knew nothing about the students, to offer constructive criticism of their work. Thus, they were always being challenged to experiment and to widen their horizons. They found it immensely stimulating: they felt Macnab's teaching and the whole atmosphere of the School drew them up to levels of achievement they had previously imagined hardly possible. They enjoyed the absence of any rigid timetable: the School was their idea of a Paris studio, where all who went, students and teachers alike, learnt from each other as well as from their own experience. They both learnt wood engraving, a wonderful way to concentrate the mind on essentials in design and pictorial composition and to strengthen dexterity and control of materials.

Winifred went on with her colour woodcuts. One she called 'London Blue' proved very popular and the whole edition sold out. 'Waterfall', another colour woodcut from this time, was bought by the Modern Arts Association. They sold well all over the country, so it is difficult now to get examples of the whole range of her work in this medium. Alison went on with design and with landscapes in oils. There was no room for a studio in Alvanley Court but they managed with the part of the living room that had been intended as the dining area. Winifred decided she would do an engraving of the view, looking north from their kitchen so she sat on the draining board with her feet in the sink, to design her 'Houses, Hampstead'.

Much of their time was spent exploring London itself: they went to galleries and encountered French art for the first time, after having been attuned to Italian schools. They found it difficult to come to terms with Cézanne when they first saw his pictures in a big exhibition devoted to his work – something Winifred remembers now with surprise. They both developed as artists in those very happy years in Alvanley Court. All the time they were teaching themselves: they would stand in front of some masterpiece in a gallery and try to analyse (had they been painting the picture) how few colours they would have had to put out on their palettes and how they would use them . . .

They went to the Victoria and Albert Museum and loved the Indian Mogul paintings. They went to the British Museum to see the Turner water colours from Petworth and when Alison moved the black covers away, which protected them from the light, 'her heart nearly stopped, they were so beautiful,' as she said to Winifred afterwards. They got student tickets for the Zoo and would practise drawing animals in movement and they and their mother were frequent visitors to Kew Gardens.

Both sisters were elected members of the National Society of Painters, Sculptors and Engravers. For this they had to submit five or six pieces of their work but then, once accepted, all subsequent work was received without question, which meant they had to keep up standards. They were also elected members of the Artist Printmakers and were regular exhibitors with the Society of Wood-Engravers, London. Winifred also exhibited with the Society of Colour Gravers. Their work was becoming known: in 1934 in the annual show of the Society of Wood Engravers in the Redfern Gallery, they were noticed as 'newcomers of much promise'. In financial terms, however, they did little more than cover their expenses with what they sold, for the galleries would take as much as sixty per cent and the cherry wood Winifred used for her colour woodcuts and the boxwood blocks for their wood engravings were expensive.

They were therefore especially grateful when they heard that an old aunt of their father had left them £250 each, and they decided to spend their legacy on another visit to Italy. This time they took their mother, and the three of them went by sea from Tilbury Docks to Naples. Winifred didn't think much of the Bay of Biscay but otherwise the holiday was sheer joy. Amalfi, in pictorial terms, was thrilling, clinging to the cliffs and as yet unspoilt by the ravages of World War II. It was on the dramatic drive over the hill that they saw home-made macaroni hanging out to dry.

Their mother in those days was almost like a sister and was able to do all sorts of things with them. She took them, for example, to Switzerland to introduce her daughters to Mlle Chevalier, who had been Principal of the school she had been sent to in Vevey.

The McKenzies had booked tickets for the open-air performance of 'Fête de Narcisses' at Montreux and asked Mlle Chevalier to go with them. She felt it was too late at night for her so she sent a young relation, Violette, to take her place, and from that time onward Violette became a life-long friend.

An exhibition of their work, held in the Cork Street Gallery, Bond Street, was well received. (One wealthy friend of their mother's came to the exhibition but was so scared that she would be expected to buy a picture that she explained as she came in, 'I've taken down all my pictures and put mirrors up instead'.) One outcome of this exhibition gave them a further field of work. Alison was commissioned to design a poster for the London North Eastern Railway, to advertise the Yorkshire Dales. The McKenzies found out that if a commissioned artist was married, the Company would pay for his wife to accompany him, so they suggested – successfully – that Winifred, as her constant companion, had an excellent claim to go with her sister.

The first of the three expeditions was in November. The weather was very cold and wet and exploring the country for suitable material meant staying in Harrogate and hiring a car. In the pouring rain they stopped for Alison to make sketches while Winifred held an umbrella over her to protect her. The railway company liked her work and next wanted a poster of the Yorkshire coast. This led to a very fruitful visit to Staithes, where they stayed in digs and were accepted at once by the fisher folk – who were accustomed to seeing painters at work, for Dame Laura Knight had been born at Staithes and grew up there. (When she became famous she moved to London and, to their bitter disappointment, never came back to see her friends.) Alison produced sketches for some of her best engravings and oil paintings there: one of them was of the 'Cod and Lobster', a very old inn, covered with pitch and frequented by the fishermen, which, sadly, has now been knocked down. Later she was to receive an appreciative letter from a distinguished fellow artist, Adrian Allinson, on the work she had done at Staithes:

'Though we have not officially met, permit me as a fellow member of the National Society to take the liberty of writing to congratulate you on your very satisfying work in the present show. I consider your "Cod and Lobster" one of the outstanding paintings of the Exhibition. Mood, colour, tone, design and feeling for volume, all unite to communicate the thrill you yourself have had and I thank you for the experience. I intend to acquire a copy of your wood engraving, which I also like very much, and I only regret my lack of means to enable me to be the owner of the painting.'

The following year the Railway people asked Alison to choose where she would like to go for her next poster. Thinking that she had never been to East Anglia, she chose the Norfolk Broads. The great skies and the sense of space delighted them but her poster *had* to be upright so she had set herself quite a challenge, which she met with an outstanding design of a windmill.

1938 was a full year for them.

In April they took part in an exhibition of 'oil paintings, watercolours, figure drawings and wood engravings including work by Tom Chadwick, Winifred and Alison McKenzie, Guy Malet, Gwenda Morgan, Rachel Reckitt and others' advertised under the title of 'Iain Macnab and His Circle'. In May they organized an exhibition of their work in Glasgow, in the Lady Artists' Club in Blythswood Square. The review in the *Glasgow Herald* spoke of the high standard of craftsmanship in the work of both artists:

'Winifred contributes a number of landscapes in colour, excellent in their tonal qualities and revealing remarkable resources in picture composition. An abstract still-life subject in oils by Winifred is outstanding in the collection. Alison shows a number of engravings – woodcuts, delicate in execution and with a sure feeling for design, while her panels in the mat oil medium for the nursery are ingeniously decorative in effect. She also shows two posters executed for the L.N.E.R . . . '

These last two were also shown in the 'Art of the Poster' exhibition in London, and a reproduction in colour of her Yorkshire coast poster was included in a catalogue for a lecture in London in 1938 on transport publicity. Earlier, her decorative map of

'Alice in Wonderland' had been shown in Bumpus Bookshop's exhibition for the centenary of Lewis Carroll. She had also been commissioned to design cards for the Ward Gallery, the Gregynog Press and the Samson Press, Oxford.

They didn't lose touch with Scotland.

Every year they were invited to stay for a fortnight in their aunt's lovely house on Loch Awe. Aunt Amy was the widow of their father's younger brother, Charlie, who had gone into the Indian Forestry Commission. He and his wife, on their journeys for the Commission, had often had to sleep in tents and forgo comforts so they used to plan together the house they would live in on the shores of Loch Awe. Unfortunately he developed dysentery so badly that they had to come home and he then caught pneumonia and died, when he was only thirty-seven. Aunt Amy, an outstandingly interesting and lovable person, had, with great courage, gone ahead and carried out the plans for their house that they had made in India. Then, each summer, members of the McKenzie family and all her own family, the Sangsters and the Dunnetts, would converge on Loch Awe and have wonderful holidays. It was very midgy, so after six o'clock no-one was to go out but instead would change into evening dress and, after dinner, they would dance and play games in her lovely drawing room. Then later, at the time of the sales, Aunt Amy would come to London, stay with the McKenzies, and enjoy shopping and going to the theatre. They would take her on expeditions, such as down to London Bridge or upriver to Hampton Court.

When, after seven years in Alvanley Court, their lease was up, they found another flat – Hamilton Court, near Maida Vale tube station. They were coming to be old London hands by now; they had certainly made the most of their opportunities in a way their father would have heartily approved. They were only a penny bus ride away from the shops on the Finchley Road. In 'John Barnes's' shop window, they noticed an advertisement that anyone who bought two pairs of stockings could have their photographs taken free – so in they went! The photographer produced chairs and his usual patter of, 'Smile please.' When it came to Alison's turn to smile, the photographer, looking up, blurted out, 'No! Don't smile! It doesn't suit you to smile!' This made Alison laugh so much that the photograph came out well.

They were halfway between the theatres at Swiss Cottage and Golders Green and became avid playgoers. Sometimes after a visit to a West End theatre, they would walk along to Piccadilly Circus in evening dress, and would watch the lights pouring Sandeman's Port into a glass, forty feet or so above the traffic, and on their return they would get out before their usual bus stop in order to walk back through the gardens.

They had no need to worry about being accosted.

In Winifred's memory of these years it was always sunny but, recalling winter, the picture of thick, white fog comes back and hearing the voices of people down below, walking beside their cars in the dark to keep the drivers from mounting the pavements. But the fogs were white, not the really choking, greasy fogs they had experienced in Glasgow.

From 1938, and especially after Munich, the prospect of war with Nazi Germany came to dominate their thoughts, and after September 1939, with the outbreak of war, Winifred and Alison decided that, for the time being, they must put away the practice of their art, though it was like cutting off a limb.

8

The First Impact of War:

September 1939 to October 1940

It was generally believed in 1939 that the first impact of war would be enemy bombing of the great cities. Since the significance of radar was not yet appreciated, and it was assumed that there was no effective defence against the bombers, the government, as well as organizing a general evacuation of primary-school children, encouraged those others who could leave London to do so.

The McKenzies received a pressing invitation from their cousin, Miss Polly Osborne of Belmore, Cupar, to join her there at the outbreak of war, so they went north in September of 1939. Miss Osborne had invited the McKenzies. She also accepted two Polish couples, each of whom had a child. One of these couples had had an amazing stroke of good fortune. When the Germans invaded Poland from the west, Krokowski had joined his unit in the army but had been swept aside by the German tank attack. Lvov, where he had left his wife, was overrun by the Russians from the east, so she decided against remaining there, under Russian rule, and moved westwards. She was pregnant. Her daughter was born in a Paris hospital but then they were moved on again, to Bordeaux this time, where they were pushed on board a ship leaving for England. And on that same ship, she found her husband: not many wartime separations ended so happily.

In addition to these nine guests, Miss Osborne also found herself hostess to ten Edinburgh evacuees – mothers and childen – for whom distraught billeting officers could find no other shelter. Belmore was only in the nature of temporary accommodation for them, but one little boy, Alastair, stayed with her for the duration.

After 1945, he went to South Africa and did very well there – and before Polly died he came back to Belmore, to thank her for all she had done for him.

As things settled down, Winifred and Alison took on ARP and other duties, but at that time, of course, these were not taxing. Part of the daily routine that developed, was listening to the six o'clock news. The only wireless was in the unheated library, so as the days got colder everyone wrapped themselves up and trooped along to listen in the dark to what was *not* happening. For these were the days of the 'phoney war', when, after the German conquest of Poland, Hitler was hoping the Allies would reach a settlement with him, while the British ministers, under Neville Chamberlain, 'were moving into war backwards with their eyes tightly closed'.

The McKenzies' lease of their Hamilton Court flat had still some time to run, and they began to feel that they shouldn't encroach on their cousin's hospitality indefinitely, so in the spring of 1940 they returned to London. It was a London of barrage balloons, blackout and petrol rationing. It was also full of troops bored with inaction, wanting to 'live it up a bit' in London and only too easily falling victim to refugees from Europe hoping to entice them into marriage so that they could take their husbands' nationality. It was to meet the need for a safe haven in London that Lady Massey, wife of the Governor General of Canada, started the Beaver Club for Canadian 'other ranks' in the former German embassy on the Mall, near Admiralty Arch. It was run by volunteers and Winifred and Alison became involved, through answering an appeal from their church to work there. The volunteers were provided with jade-green overalls, and badges for those with special responsibilities, so that the soldiers would know they were helpers (not predators).

Dunkirk and the fall of France changed the whole atmosphere in London and through the Beaver Club – as well as Canadians – came those rescued from the Dunkirk beaches, British and Free French; soldiers, sailors and airmen. Winifred was on the reception desk to welcome the men and take their names, which she would put into the appropriately lettered pigeon hole behind her. The Information Bureau was in another room, where there were many helpers. This was where Alison worked. Her job was to build up a reference book, which would make information readily available to the men: on where they were being offered hospitality, for instance, or what form of transport was available – answers to the hundred and one questions with which she was bombarded every day. She was also getting into order the details that the men gave about their families and backgrounds . . . It was very valuable work and Alison was making a good job of it, with her orderly mind and ability to concentrate.

The task of making out the duty rotas was handed over to Winifred and Alison, each on their own side of the running of the club; so they got to know all the helpers. Scotland Yard alerted them to a danger they found it very difficult at first to grasp: that some of the helpers were deliberately trying to undermine the morale of the troops, or, if not deliberately, then they were being used by others to spread defeatist propaganda. And it was to those others that Scotland Yard needed a lead.

Because Winifred and Alison knew a certain amount of French, Canadian French and Free French tended to be referred to them. Once at the end of May (1940), when some of the Free French airmen were visiting them at Hamilton Court, they took them up on to their flat roof, to look at London. As it happened, the barrage balloons were going up for the coming night, and one of the Frenchmen remarked to the others:

'You know I believe Britain's in earnest. France will never stick it out.'

One afternoon, a 'pearly king' from Petticoat Lane Market, a real old costermonger with his coat splendidly covered with pearl buttons, arrived at Winifred's desk, asking if somebody called 'Vines' had registered with the Club. He explained that the people at the Market had told him that a Canadian had been asking for 'Vines' but the Market knew the 'pearly king' and his sister as 'the Wags', so couldn't help. Winifred looked up the file, discovered there was a Vines there, so she got in touch with the BBC and the 'pearly king' found that the young soldier was the son of his brother, who had gone out to Canada years ago and hadn't been heard of since.

Alison, in the Information Bureau, was asked by a sailor, a young boy from the Canadian prairies, if he could get any clothes because his ship had been torpedoed. She asked him why he'd joined the Navy and he said he had thought it would be cleaner! Having been given both clothes and a proper meal, he then remarked in a vague way: 'I know I have relatives in London but my address book went down with ship'. He added that his relative's name was Robertson and that he was in the London Police Force. As it happened, Alison was at that moment in touch with Scotland Yard, and when she had dealt with her point, thought it worth adding: 'There's a boy here with relatives named Robertson, one of whom is in the London Police Force.' The Scotland Yard man roared with laughter and said: 'There are *pages* of Robertsons in the London police – but wait a minute, there's a chap working here in this office who said something about Canadian relatives' . . . And it turned out it was the right Robertson! The young sailor came back, with an enormous box of chocolates for Alison, to tell her:

'Not only did I find an uncle and aunt but fourteen cousins . . . and, I had a whale of a holiday.'

So one way and another Winifred and Alison found themselves needed the whole of each day at the Beaver Club, during that momentous summer of 1940, and they really helped to keep things going in an orderly way, amid a flutter of Society ladies who hadn't had the discipline of that kind of work before.

In their flat in Hamilton Court they were feeling the impact of war with increasing severity. Rationing of food had been organized since January; their windows were stuck across with tape to minimize the effect of glass splintering through bomb blast; their buckets of sand and water were at the ready to put out fires. Their father's brother, Ken, and their mother's sister, Amy, had been forced to leave Jersey when the Channel Islands were occupied by the Germans. They found that the flat on the floor below the McKenzies at Hamilton Court could be rented, and they moved in there.

(The Germans used Uncle Ken's Jersey house as an officers' club but never discovered the case of whisky which, at the last moment, he had dug into his dung heap, or the valuable cameras and telescopes, etc, which he had hidden beneath a trap-door under the table at which the officers dined every day. The Germans withdrew hastily at the end of the war and Uncle Ken had the satisfaction not only of finding his own buried treasures but in redistributing all the goods belonging to other islanders which he had discovered in his garage. They had been collected there by the Germans who hadn't left time to take them away.)

During the late summer of 1940 the Battle of Britain was fought out between the RAF and the Luftwaffe. The crucial phase of the battle was when the Germans set out to destroy the bases of Fighter Command in Kent and very nearly succeeded. Air Marshal Dowding, directing operations and desperately short of trained pilots, had grave cause for anxiety. Then, on 7 September, this was miraculously relieved: the Germans turned aside to bomb London – so when, early in the morning of 8 September, Winifred went up on to the roof of Hamilton Court and saw the red glow of London docks burning, it meant that the Kent airfields were saved and that the Germans would never get command of the Channel for long enough to launch their invasion of Britain. But it also meant the beginning of the 'Blitz' on London. Every night until November, about half an hour after it got dark, Londoners heard the characteristic drone of German planes, the firing of ack-ack guns, the patter of shrapnel and then the explosion of bombs.

The sirens would wail, swooping up and down in a dismal way, when German planes were reported to be approaching London, and at first the people's reaction to them was fairly insouciant. As a friend said: 'I don't worry at all. I just collect my book and a bottle of sherry and go to the shelter.' But the warnings became more and more frequent so different tactics had to be adopted. As there was no shelter at Hamilton Court, the people in the flats took their quilts down to the entrance hall and slept – or tried to sleep – there, lying bundled up so close to each other that they had to tell their neighbours when they were going to turn over. They heard one little boy say to his mother: 'Oh mummy – tell the porter to sound the All-Clear now; I'm tired.'

Their night-porter proved a tower of strength. When a Molotov cocktail (a sort of basket firebomb which on impact would scatter its fiery contents in all directions) dropped on their roof, it was he who, with the ARP wardens, prevented the young people from rushing about, and then put out the numerous small fires. Another time they had a direct hit on their gas main which meant a flame of gas burning to illuminate their bulding. It took a long time to put it out and even longer to get back anything like steady or adequate gas pressure. They would light their gas stove and be cheered by the flame, but only too quickly it would lose heart and sink to the merest peep. Winifred remembers hearing one woman say to her neighbour:

'Can you make a stew nowadays?'

And the answer came:

'Oh, yes! It only takes two days!'

Then, abruptly, Winifred's and Alison's work at the Beaver Club came to an end. Alison had wanted to get on more quickly with compiling the reference book (which was very much needed) but found it difficult to do so, working at the counter, when the men were always leaning on it to show their photographs or look at maps of London and so on. The last thing she wanted was to discourage them so she asked her immediate superior if she could possibly work at a table behind the counter. Alison, the last person to throw her weight about, was thinking only of the task she wanted to get on with – it needed doing and she was the one best able to do it well. Of course, Alison did not have a title and her superior appeared to place great value on a titles. The upshot was that she decided Alison was getting 'too big for her boots', and she actually said to Winifred:

'A table is a special privilege for titled people, and I've told Alison we can do without her.'

It was a sorry end to a period of valuable and rewarding work for both of them and it left them feeling rather winded, as if they had been given a punch in the solar plexus.

They suddenly had to rethink their whole situation but they got down to it and the three of them concluded that there was no longer much point in staying on at Hamilton Court. Winifred and Alison knew that their mother was very short of sleep and the nights were getting noisier and the conditions more impossible. They decided they would go north, this time to St Andrews. They would stay in the St Rule Club until they found a place of their own. So they made the journey north – a twelve-hour trial of endurance in war time – and during their very first night in St Andrews, 25 October, they heard the familiar drone of a German plane overhead and the explosion of German bombs; more falling on St Andrews that night than at any other time in the war.

Through an advertisement they saw in Macfarlane's, the grocer's shop, they found a flat in Playfair Terrace – Number 4 – only temporary, but it gave them a breathing space to look for a permanent base.

Winifred with Annabel Kidston

At one of the exhibitions of the work of the class for the forces which
had been started by Winifred and Annabel. These exhibitions were
held in the Lower College Hall, St Salvator's, St Andrews.

9

The War Years for Winifred:

St Andrews, 1940–5

The first year of the war had brought the McKenzie sisters into exhilarating but fleeting contact with many hundreds of Canadians in London. The remaining years saw them (but particularly Winifred, because Alison joined the ATS), deeply involved with much smaller numbers of the Forces; Polish, British, Norwegian . . . but in a way which forged friendships still surviving fifty years after the end of the war.

The question of where to live in St Andrews was settled when Number 3, Playfair Terrace was put on the market. The McKenzies on their arrival had linked up with Annabel Kidston, who was, like them, a member of the Artists Printmakers and whose work they had already seen in exhibitions. Annabel's sister, Nell, wanted her own place and was ready to join with Mary McKenzie in buying and dividing Number 3. Nell wanted the garden so she had the basement and ground floor, the McKenzies the two top floors and responsibility for the roof. In its existing condition, the house, apart from a plethora of wash-hand basins because of it having been a hotel, was not particularly convenient, with the bathroom poised halfway between the two floors and the kitchen created from a back bedroom, with a second-hand gas stove and a sink which the McKenzies had managed to acquire but no room to put anything down (though there was always the floor). But the flat was central and gave them a sense of light and space, especially on the south side overlooking the road.

They found that St Andrews was playing host to many Polish Servicemen who had been sent to defend the east coast of Scotland

against invasion. The people of St Andrews had organized canteens for the troops and were ready to welcome the Poles into their
homes, but what these young men needed was something besides
soldiering on which to exercise their minds and use their talents.
As Mr Thomson of Fairfield Stores said:

'What these boys need is education, not just tea and scones.'

This chimed with what Winifred and Alison were thinking: that
they could use their experience to teach drawing and engraving to
those who would like to learn in their leisure time.

Once again they consulted Annabel, who proved to be co-
operative and full of ideas. Another of her sisters, Margaret
Kidston, an assistant lecturer in the university, and Mr Snodgrass,
in charge of Adult Education for the Forces, became their allies in
finding a place to meet and funding for the proposed classes.

The University authorities agreed to let them have a room above
Upper College Hall, part of the Psychology Department's domain.
This was approached first by the wide staircase at the east end of
the Lower College Hall and then by a rather dark spiral one up
from there to a room which was permanently blacked out. On the
funding side, the Committee for Adult Education allocated enough
money to enable them to get sufficient equipment – more, that, is
than the locked cupboard and the few tables and chairs already
there. They managed to buy some anglepoise lamps and drawing
boards and, from T.N. Lawrence of London, they bought as many
wood-engraving blocks, tools and the special paper needed, as
wartime shortages would allow. It was not enough, so they had
their own blocks resurfaced for their pupils. The men had to pay
for the blocks and, on a shilling a day, this was not easy, but none
of them ever defaulted.

It was actually in December 1940 that Winifred and Annabel put
up notices about the classes in the YMCA and the local canteens
for the Forces. The response the first night was overwhelming:
there were those who came for a lark, those who thought they
might as well try their hand at something fresh, and those prepared
to be serious students. None of them had ever done any engraving
before but, as it became clear to the men that their supervisors were

professional artists as well as dedicated teachers, they responded with enthusiasm and appreciated the friendly atmosphere in the class, as did the Earl of Haddington. The first time he came – in his RAF uniform with all his ribbons – Winifred asked him if he had come to inspect the men. 'Good Lord, no! I've come to join the class!' he replied and thereafter came round regularly from the Grand Hotel (now Hamilton Hall) where he was in charge of the Air Force cadets.

As many of the students were Poles, the problem of language was acute at first. One of the Poles gave Winifred a *Teach Yourself Polish*. She tried. The result caused a lot of merriment. She then got lessons from Captain Stach Krynski, a former professor in Warsaw, and with his help she read several books in Polish. Being able to understand the written word proved invaluable when later dealing with letters from Poland about members of her class who had been reported missing or killed.

Winifred and Annabel were also asked to go over to Dundee to start a wood-engraving class for the Forces there. Again the men who joined it soon realized what a great opportunity they had to learn under teachers who treated them as human beings and really wanted them to do good work. One of these was Otto Macaig from Poland, who was in an ack-ack unit defending Dundee. Later he was posted to St Andrews and joined the art class there as well. He remembers Winifred's teaching as the most valuable experience he had in the war. It gave him the confidence to go on to Art College after the war and to take up teaching art at Monmouth Grammar School, which he made his career until his recent retirement. He has always kept in touch with Winifred and remembers with great affection his visits to 3b Playfair Terrace and the warm welcome which the McKenzies always gave these young boys.

Many of the class, especially the Poles, proved to have very considerable artistic gifts, and learnt quickly. Among these were Ewaryst Jakubowski, Klocek and Sterling. They were outstanding students, who would never have met and formed their close friendships, had it not been for the class – being, as they were, all from different units: one an engineer, one a signalman, and the third from the infantry. In 1942 these three were asked by their commanding officers to produce ideas for a memorial which would commemorate the Polish role as defenders of St Andrews during the years when invasion threatened. They decided on a mosaic, though they had never attempted anything in that line before. But on one of their leaves, when they had gone together into Edinburgh, they had met a lecturer from the College of Art there, and from him they had every expectation of receiving help. They worked out a design, which was accepted, and were given leave to go into Edinburgh to carry it out.

It was very disheartening therefore to find their lecturer ill in hospital but he told them from his sick bed where to go for materials and gave them advice on the essential techniques. They needed space for their work and were given an empty, high-ceilinged room at the top of a house, with a skylight and access to the roof. They set to work with all the confidence of youth and asked Winifred and Annabel if they would come over and give them their reaction to what they had done so far. It was a visit they always remembered: seeing the work taking shape. They asked if they could look at it from further away so the five of them climbed out onto the roof to look through the skylight at it. The men were worried that they had used the word 'City' because it fitted the space better than 'Town', so Winifred and Annabel were able to reassure them that the use of 'Town' would have offended the people of the 'Royal Burgh of St Andrews'.

The mosaic was finished within the six weeks for which they had been given leave, brought over to St Andrews in a lorry, inserted into the west wall of the Town Hall and unveiled with all due ceremony. This included the presentation of a scroll to the Provost, which recorded the Polish Forces' presence in St Andrews. The three young artists wanted to make sure that there was a Polish eagle somewhere in their handiwork so they cut a cherry woodblock as a mould, melted sealing-wax on the McKenzies' gas stove, and made a seal to affix to the scroll. And with its legend, *Polish Soldier to St Andrews City*, the mosaic *has* fulfilled the purpose for which it was designed — that is, in General Jan Paszkiewicz's words:

'To be, for future generations, a visible symbol of our stay in your country.'

The presence of Poles billeted in the Ardgowan Hotel next door to 3b gave Winifred another vivid memory of the years they were in St Andrews. Every morning they would assemble in the garden of the Ardgowan and she would hear them singing in Polish:

Kiedy ranne wstają zorze
Tobie ziemia, Tobie morze,
Tobie śpiewa żywiot wszelki,
Bądź pochwalon Boże Wielki.

When in the morning the dawn arises,
To you the earth, to you the sea,
To you all living creatures give their praises:
May God be praised!

The Poles always sang too when they were marching.

Knowing from experience how valuable it had proved when Iain Macnab, at the Grosvenor School of Modern Art, had insisted that all work should be framed, Winifred and Annabel mounted the men's work for them and kept a record of all they did. This helped in organizing exhibitions, which the men found most encouraging, especially when their prints were sold. Otto Macaig was recently (summer 1995) in London to visit a Polish professor who had come back here to live, and as Otto was going up the stairs, he was moved to see one of his own wartime wood engravings which the professor had kept and must have valued.

Annabel Kidston was Winifred's constant and doughty ally. She took the lead on the public relations side and was infinitely resourceful when it came to mounting exhibitions. For instance, on several occasions the University authorities gave them permission to use Lower College Hall to show the men's work but with the proviso that nothing whatever should be stuck anywhere into the walls. So Annabel went over to Newport where she knew someone who could provide hessian, brought back as much as she could manage and then she and Winifred successfully pinned up the mounts on the draped hessian.

It was she who suggested that the National Gallery of Scotland in Edinburgh should be asked if they would put on an exhibition of the work the members of the Forces had done in St Andrews. They agreed, and the exhibition was organized in May of 1943. There were twenty-eight Polish works and seventeen from British soldiers and, accompanying these, photographs of the classes in session. A notice in the *Evening Dispatch* about the exhibition, commented on the vivacity of the work and the 'remarkably high standard of execution' considering the amateur status of the exhibitors and that they could only attend the classes in their leisure time. The notice also praised the arrangement of the work by which the various stages in the development of the artist, from simple blocks to imaginative figure compositions, could be seen.

It was Annabel too who provided an unexpected wartime feast for herself and the McKenzies. One particularly dark night she came out from her house in Market Street to go to the class, and tripped over something soft. Picking it up she discovered it was a pheasant, which was obviously intended for somebody's table but must have fallen off a bicycle. She reported her find at the Police Station where the officer on duty took a very practical view:

'Keep it five days if you must,' he said, handing the bird back to Annabel. 'But for Heaven's sake don't give it to us because we have to keep it nine months!'

So the pheasant was made the occasion of a celebratory feast – it was getting near Christmas – the only slight hitch being with the mince pies afterwards. Annabel was not an attentive or very interested cook, and, not noticing that her domestic help had tidied up her larder, mixed in a liberal helping of what she thought were currants into the mincemeat, only to discover at her party that they weren't currants at all but peppercorns.

The McKenzies wished to help Ewaryst Jakubowski: he wanted to get a direct message through to his mother to tell her he was alive. He talked over with the McKenzies whether there was any possibility of getting such a message through. They were in touch with Violette, their Swiss friend in Vevey, whom they had known for many years, and they also knew that the Swiss Red Cross had some lines of communication with Poland, so they thought it was worth a try. Ewaryst wrote his letter in his own hand, to Violette, and signed it 'Winifred and Alison'. It was on the lines of:

'Do you remember the wonderful holiday we had together in Poland? Do you remember Maria who lived [the address followed] . . . ? We are wondering how she is.'

Violette had no idea what it was all about – she knew the McKenzies had never been to Poland – but she played her part and so did the Red Cross, and they heard later that the message did get through. They explained to a mystified Violette after the war what it had all been about.

In 1943 Ewaryst took the grave decision to volunteer to para-chute back into Poland to join the Resistance, and went off to train for this. He left his belongings and a letter for his family with the McKenzies.

He succeeded in getting to Warsaw and made for his cousin's house and there by a chance, which both of them blessed, he met his brother Konrad, who, a regular soldier, had been unable to get away from Wilno. They had just that one night together and spent it talking. (To stay longer would have endangered their cousin's life even further.) Konrad had had horrific adventures. He had joined the underground movement and been captured by the Gestapo, who, after beating him up, sent him to a labour camp. The prisoners were put to cutting down trees and when a branch fell on him he pretended to be more concussed than he really was, and so was taken to hospital. From there he managed to escape and made his way to Warsaw where, for that one night, he met and talked with his younger brother.

After that meeting, Konrad managed to make his way to France and survived by helping French farmers bury their treasure in exchange for food and shelter until the Americans arrived. He was then sent to the Polish Headquarters in London and from there posted on to Scotland. On his first leave he made for St Andrews to give the McKenzies news of Ewaryst, who had talked much of them and of St Andrews, on that one night of their meeting. On a later leave after the end of the war, Konrad was again in St Andrews, helping Winifred and Annabel to clear out everything from their room in the Psychology Department. As he emerged into the quadrangle, someone came up to him to bring him news of his brother: Ewaryst had been killed fighting in the sewers in the Warsaw Rising. Full of memories of his brother, Konrad went round to the mosaic in Queen's Gardens and left there a single carnation on the pavement below. The mosaic was, after all, something Ewaryst had helped to create.

Konrad stayed in Scotland and finished his engineering training before returning to Poland, where he married. But the link forged with the McKenzies during the war has never been broken. Konrad took great pleasure in sending Winifred and Alison red roses at Christmas and letters were still regularly exchanged until his recent death.

The second of the 'mosaic trio', Klocek, was also dropped by air into Poland in 1943 to join the resistance movement. No news was heard of him, and at the end of the war Winifred wrote to Polish Headquarters in London, but all that they could tell her was that he was officially 'missing'. So Winifred sent his personal belongings to his mother in Zakopane. But she resented not knowing what had happened to her son and, brooding over her loss, became convinced that there must be some clue in St Andrews which would help her find him.

So ten years after the end of the war she wrote to Winifred asking her to come to meet her in London and escort her up to St Andrews. But this was simply not possible for Winifred at that point, with her teaching in Dundee and her mother an invalid, and Pani Klocek knew no English. So Winifred asked Jozef Sekalski, a fellow artist in St Andrews, to write explaining to Pani Klocek why Winifred couldn't get to London at that point and why a search in St Andrews would be a hopeless quest. The distraught mother sent a terrible letter in reply, bitterly reproaching Winifred, so Jozef

Sekalski suggested that she tear the letter up as if she had never received it. She did this and continued to send Christmas greetings each year.

But Pani Klocek still didn't give up.

After another ten years Konrad was in Afghanistan on an engineering project, and was sent a Polish magazine. In it was a letter from Pani Klocek appealing for news of her son and giving an account of his time in St Andrews and a photograph of the Polish mosaic. It prompted Klocek to go to see his mother. Konrad wrote to Winifred from Afghanistan to tell her he had seen *another* letter from Pani Klocek, in the next issue of the magazine, a triumphant one this time, thanking the magazine for having helped to put her in touch with her son. Klocek also wrote once to Winifred and she could see by the distinctive handwriting that it was indeed the Klocek she had known. But there were no other letters and she learned nothing of what had happened in the intervening twenty years.

Jan Sterling's link was closer to the Kidstons than to the McKenzies. He went to Liverpool after the war to take an architectural training, at which he did brilliantly, and Winifred and Annabel went down to Liverpool to see him receive his degree. He went off to America and nothing more was heard of him until at the end of 1982, when Winifred was preparing Alison's memorial exhibition and had gone to the Town Hall about her St Andrews' poster.

The clerkess there apologised for having to go but she had promised to meet a friend from Boston, Mass. about photographing the Polish mosaic. The friend had been asked by an old man in Boston who lived down her street, if she would take a photograph of it because he had helped in its making. Winifred realized, of course, that this must be Sterling.

It was only in 1988 that Maronski, who had also been a member of Winifred's class and had stayed on in St Andrews, brought her a copy of the Polish paper published in Britain in which he had noticed an obituary of Sterling, probably by someone who had been a student with him in Liverpool. It spoke of his successful architectural career in Boston and the development of his distinctive style, of his high reputation as a painter and sculptor, of the beautiful house overlooking the Atlantic which he had built for himself and his American wife, of the Arms of Warsaw he had sculpted and painted and put above his front door.

Winifred had not been 'called up' as Alison had been, because one of them had to stay with their mother who was becoming more of an invalid. So, with looking after her mother, keeping house, keeping the wood engraving and art classes going, she was pretty well at full stretch the whole time.

10

The War Years for Alison, 1940–6

The British people were more fully mobilized in the Second World War than those of any other nation and Alison knew that she would have to make difficult choices when her call-up came. Till then she helped Winifred and Annabel with their classes in the evenings and looked round for a daytime job. She was in the bank, asking if they needed any clerical help, when Mr Gilchrist – of the law firm Ritchie, Doig and Gilchrist – unexpectedly stopped in his tracks and murmured an enquiry: did she know anything about income tax? 'Does anyone?' was Alison's answer, but since there seemed to be a plea for help here, she followed him upstairs to his office. This was the most uninhibitedly paper-strewn room she had ever seen, but Mr Gilchrist knew what he wanted: someone to spend time listening to his clients and helping them sort out their financial concerns.

In this casual way, Alison found herself applying her mind to income tax and all branches of work dealing with the factoring of estates. It was an entirely new field for her and the way she took to it showed again how intelligent and clear-minded she was. Mr Gilchrist, in the testimonial he wrote for her when she left to go into the Forces, said:

'In a surprisingly short time she not only mastered the main part of her work but suggested and adopted improved methods of keeping records and returns . . . Her work was of a responsible nature and included personal interviews with exacting clients who were very pleased with her efficient handling of all their business.'

Indeed she soon realized that many of those who came to her wanted more than financial advice: they wanted a listening ear and a sympathetic voice to give them the chance to blow off steam or help them tackle problems they would rather have avoided.

In June 1943 she received her call-up papers. The first suggestion put to her was work in a Glasgow munitions factory. She decided against that and so was called for an interview to see about joining the Forces. A comfortable body, sitting with her back to a nice fire, began by asking if her father was in the Navy? No? Well, what about the RAF? Perhaps she was engaged to an airman? Alison had again to say no – but offered to get a fiancé for the weekend if it would help. This was brushed aside as too frivolous and judgement was pronounced: Alison could go at once into the ATS – and so she did, at the age of thirty-six, which meant she was much older than any of the other girls.

She was put into uniform and into a hut with sixteen others, only two of whom had clean heads. Mr Gilchrist had spoken in his testimonial, of Alison's 'faculty of getting on well with people in all stations of life with whom she may come in contact'. He was right in this too. She found it a bit startling at first when tea was brought in in a bucket with milk and sugar already added, but once she realized the drill, she dipped her mug in with the rest and generally set herself to make friends with the others and prove to them – and herself – that she would tackle without demur all the menial jobs allotted to them. Sometimes there were advantages to being on the kitchen front. She learned that while the officers upstairs might be sitting in a chilly room and eating their margarine ration on their bread, being with the cooks meant lots of butter and a seat by a warm fire. It was while she was a private that she especially appreciated the peaceful haven that she always found in the Salvation Army hut.

What angered her was the attitude of some of those in authority in the Services. For instance, she caught a very bad dose of flu and had to go to hospital. The doctor in charge of her ward made all the patients stand to attention, in an inadequately heated building, while she carried out an inspection, in spite of the fact that some of the girls were fainting.

Whenever it could be arranged, Alison would meet Winifred in

Edinburgh and of course, go home when she had leave. Anyway she battled on and after nine months in the ranks, she was persuaded she ought to take her WOSB – the War Office Selection Board – and was sent to Yorkshire for five days of gruelling tests. She had a streaming cold and the first hurdle was a cross-country run, not her favourite occupation at the best of times. After that she had to submit to various psychological tests and was pressed hard on the subject of why she wasn't engaged. She found it all rather distasteful.

She had then to make a five-minute speech, in front of the Board, on a subject picked out of a hat. It was: 'What advice would you give your girls if an American contingent was stationed nearby?' It wasn't a straightforward question: she tried to get the balance between warning them to beware of the glamour of free-spending, attractive strangers and reminding them that these newcomers were our guests and that we desperately needed the help they could bring.

When Winifred met her off the train on her return, she was exhausted and remarked ruefully: 'I'm definitely not the stuff officers are made of.' But of the twenty-seven who had gone up, five were chosen and Alison was one of them. She wore her white cadet tabs for the requisite time and then was made a second subaltern and sent to Glencorse. It was here she met Elizabeth Young, as her commanding officer, and this made all the difference to the rest of her time at Glencorse. Elizabeth and Alison were put in charge of the cooks and orderlies and what amazed them about 'their girls' was their total lack of self-restraint, especially when it came to their boyfriends. If they thought they were being stood up or someone else was poaching, they would throw themselves down on their beds in a frenzy of noisy yelling and crying. Elizabeth and Alison were the only two women in the Mess among browned-off officers, mostly doctors, who were fed up and bored because they knew they hadn't been selected for the active service abroad which was impending. They drank heavily, so dinners in the Mess were a trial and the silly pranks afterwards rather disgusting.

The first time Alison was on duty after she became an officer began rather alarmingly. She was woken up at night to be told that there was a girl attacking the cook with a knife and would she please come? The girl was fighting drunk and had a very quick temper but somehow Alison sorted things out and got everybody to bed. About a month later, the girl who had caused the stir, asked Alison:

'Ma'am, would you give me away at the altar?'

Not only did Alison do that but she also managed to get a cake for what turned out to be a happy wedding party. Another girl, who had two brothers in prison, and whom people tended to look down on, was the one who had enough fellow-feeling with Alison to bring her tea when she heard that Alison had got back from her brother Alec's funeral.

Alison was in charge of paying the girls, so every month she had to go into Edinburgh, get the money and thumb a lift back to Glencorse. (On one occasion she tried – unavailingly – to persuade the driver of a hearse to take her back to camp.) It never seems to have entered Alison's or anyone else's head that she might be at risk carrying all that money.

Edinburgh can be a cold place, and Glencorse on the edge of Edinburgh, seemed to Alison that winter (1944–5) to be positively arctic. It was partly that they were billeted in a big, draughty, unheated, nineteenth-century house, with no carpets, very little furniture and a quite inadequate hot-water supply. Hers was not a particularly strong constitution at the best of times, and being always tensed with the cold (having in fact to undress at night beneath the bedclothes in order to preserve her existing heat), made her less able to resist infection. She was taken ill with hepatitis and if Elizabeth had not been there to realize how ill Alison was and get her to hospital, things might have gone very badly indeed with her. As it was, she was four months in hospital but this time she was blessed with a first-rate and most understanding doctor.

Alison was promoted to Junior Commander – the equivalent in the ATS of the rank of Captain. Having asked not to be sent abroad, she was posted to Windsor, where she was made to realize that fainting on parade was an offence very nearly warranting imprisonment in the Tower!

As the war was coming to an end, she was made an education officer and sent on a course to St Andrews, which proved a delight-ful week's change, with the pleasure of seeing her family at 3b. Her last posting was to Newbattle Abbey as rehabilitation officer where she organized courses in cookery and domestic science and classes which would get the girls back to thinking like civilians. Her great difficulty was finding materials for them to work with. She did her best and actually managed to get some wood engraving blocks, one of which she used to produce a Christmas card for Newbattle.

The visit of 'Monty' (Field Marshal Montgomery) to Newbattle was carefully prepared for; in spite of the headline in the *Evening News*: 'ATS officer surprised by Army Chief,' over a photograph of Alison, working on a woodblock with Monty looking over her shoulder. He did in fact show some interest in the process of engraving so she tried to explain briefly the various stages.

Alison was demobilized in 1946 after three years in the Army. It had been another testing period – different sorts of tests altogether from anything that had gone before – but she had come through them and Winifred remembered thinking that, after her return to civilian life, 'she had a richer laugh.'

The Woodcut Monty Saw

This is the Christmas card featuring Newbattle Abbey which Alison
was working on when Field Marshal Montgomery visited.

11

Dundee College of Art, 1944–57

In 1944 with the shift of Allied Forces to the south of England for D–Day and the return to Europe, Winifred's St Andrews class came to an end. It was Annabel Kidston who drew her attention to an advertisement from the Dundee College of Art asking for applications for someone to teach screen printing. When Winifred pointed out that she had not done any screen printing and therefore could hardly teach it, Annabel suggested that she should apply anyway and take over some of her engravings and wood cuts. This she did and after her interview, was appointed to the staff of the College as lecturer in composition, life drawing and wood engraving. She would be an innovator here because wood engraving had not before been taught in Dundee.

The Principal of the College at this time was Francis Cooper, who had been appointed back in 1927 when the terms of the Duncan of Jordanstone Bequest were being fiercely argued over by its trustees: the Board of Management of the Technical College, Dundee Town Council, the *Courier and Advertiser* and the Educational Endowments Commission for Scotland. Cooper had used all his influence to keep the goal of a separate College of Art in its own new buildings before the public, with no rumours of indiscipline or bohemian behaviour by the students to deter support. That battle had been won in the 1930s and only the outbreak of the second World War prevented a beginning being made on the new building in the Perth Road, yet Cooper's principal concern still seems to have centred on matters of discipline.

He need have had no anxiety on that score. Through being taught by Iain Macnab, Winifred had learnt how to engage the interest of students and encourage them to express their views and have them treated seriously. And four years of teaching members of the Forces had made her confident that she could, as a teacher, get on terms with men quite as well as with women.

What might perhaps have engaged the attention of the College authorities in more detail was making the best use of the ludicrously overcrowded conditions for the art students in the Bell Street buildings. Winifred found that sometimes there was simply nowhere for her class to work in college, so she would take them out: to the docks, to the Caird Hall where they sat at the upstairs windows, to the Howff. Even this was not without its complications – not concerned with discipline, as Principal Cooper might have feared – but with the prior claims of someone's horse to the grass the students were sitting on between the grave stones. Winifred was in no position to argue with the irate owner of the horse, when he appeared, so she had to tell her students to pack up their things and leave him in possession of the field.

In actual fact, the challenge this sort of difficulty set both staff and students evoked a very positive response from them all, and those returning from the Forces and then from National Service were mature and more strongly motivated than those who later on came straight from school.

Alison was demobilized in 1946 and would have liked a full-time job but she and Winifred had to take the health of their mother into consideration. It would certainly not be good for her to be left alone all day. In the end they decided to ask the College authorities if it would be possible for them to divide Winifred's job between them, teaching the same students – the third years – and drawing one salary. This was agreed, so the new regime started with only one of them making her way each weekday to the St Andrews railway station for the simple, half-hour journey to Dundee.

Mr Cooper seems to have had no worries about Alison's ability to keep the students in order – had she not been a Junior Commander in the ATS? She first joined the design staff but very soon felt she could be more use on the drawing and painting side. Here she would have been much happier had she been asked to teach still life instead of the drawing and painting of heads and this in a room where, through failure to consult the staff, the lighting was all wrong. It was stuck high up on the ceiling and cast dark shadows under the eyes of the models and under their cheek bones in the most distorting way.

Alison, like Winifred, proved to be a good teacher. They worked in great harmony together but each had her own individual approach to drawing and painting and their students valued the different insights each contributed in their teaching. The fact that they had the same third-year students meant that they could really get to know them and decide between themselves how individual students could best be helped.

Many who are now distinguished look back to the challenge of their Bell Street days and acknowledge the satisfaction it gave them to overcome the difficulties. They form a remarkable lot who have remained friends with Winifred to this day. To mention only a few: the painters, William Littlejohn, Irene Halliday, Ann Patrick, William Cadenhead; Morris Grassie, who became Director of Art at Moray House; Stewart Bannerman, who was the designer of the recent wood panels in St Mary's Church, Dundee; David Walker, Chief Inspector of Historic Buildings; and Angus Gallon, who was Chief Inspector of Art in Scottish Schools.

In 1950 Alberto Morrocco came from Aberdeen to be head of Drawing and Painting at the College. His gifts as a painter helped to emphasize the status of Dundee as a college with a very high standard of painting.

In 1953 Mr Gray, the then President of the RSW, saw Alison's work when he was visiting Dundee and was so impressed that he suggested she should send examples of her painting to the Society. As a result she was made a member, which helped her position as a painter.

Also in that year, the foundation stone of the new separate College of Art was laid at the Perth Road site, and Francis Cooper retired as Principal. But Winifred and Alison never taught in the new building they had been hearing about ever since they began in Dundee, because their mother was now needing much more nursing: they had to resign.

What was a source of great satisfaction to them was that their place was taken by two artists of real distinction – David McClure, on the painting side, and Jozef Sekalski – to develop in the new buildings the wood engraving Winifred had begun.

On Holiday with Violette Dufour

The sisters relaxing with their Swiss friend Violette (centre).

12

Back to Painting, 1957–66

Until 1957 the opportunities for the McKenzie sisters to get back to their own painting were limited by their teaching in Dundee and increasingly, between 1957 and 1966, by the nursing they needed to give their mother. Over this period she became increasingly frail physically but mentally she was as strong-minded as ever. If she didn't approve of a project:

'No!' she would say. 'Over my dead body . . . '

But with judicious cups of tea her daughters usually managed to get done what they felt was really necessary. For instance, they needed better light in the room on the top floor they were trying to use as their studio. It only had one narrow dormer window in the roof and as the easel *had* to be at the highest point of the coom-ceiling, if Winifred was painting a still-life, then Alison had to sit behind her to get any light at all. They therefore asked their mother if they could have roof lights put in. She at once envisaged a major building undertaking: tiles off, timbers brought up the stairs, noise, clutter, leaks round the new window frames . . . so her immediate reaction was a firm, 'Over my dead body . . . ' But soon after this two roof lights were put in, the job took only one day, and their mother was as delighted as they were at the way the new lighting transformed the room into a studio.

The telephone on the top floor, to save them having to run down twenty steps to answer it, was another idea which needed cups of tea. 'What do you want now?' their mother would ask with a twinkle, her suspicions aroused. Again she was envisaging holes knocked in the plaster work and dust and mess. When the telephone too proved a simple operation, they would hear her telling her friends that she was so glad she had thought of it.

Another of her vigorous phrases: 'A man running for his life would never see that . . . ' was used to brush aside her daughters' mild criticism of her untidiness and she would point out that she knew where everything was, which was quite true. And they knew she was devoted to their interests: she was tremendously pleased for instance when the Duke of Edinburgh bought Winifred's oil painting 'The Blue Table' at the 1963 summer exhibition at the Royal Scottish Academy.

After they gave up teaching in 1957, Roberta Sekalska, who had trained at the Slade and was teaching art at St Leonards School, suggested that they should join her and her husband, Jozef Sekalski and his Polish friend at the Bell Rock House down at the harbour, for painting sessions in her studio. Jozef had, with great hardship, escaped from Poland but had not been able to make his way to Britain until later than the younger Poles with whom Winifred had worked. He was already an experienced artist: a brilliant wood engraver with a style all his own, and also a most distinguished calligrapher. His wartime experiences had undermined his health – smugglers had helped him over the mountains in the snow, whence he had made his way to Budapest. There, with the help of the Red Cross, he had sold the prints he had brought with him and with the money thus raised continued his westward journey. Settled in St Andrews, he managed to get a teaching post at New Park School and he and Roberta decided to get married. The ceremony was carried out very quietly at the Bell Rock House, with Janet Macfarlane, headmistress of St Leonards, and Mary McKenzie as their two witnesses.

Thus it was a small, closely-knit group which got down to work in Roberta's studio. If they needed a model, they shared the expense; what they chiefly prized was the stimulus of each other's company and the shared sense of the worthwhileness of what they were about. The McKenzies valued the discussions with Jozef on painting and the discipline of art.

They had no car so they acquired a cross between a pram and

a pushcart, which somehow came to be called 'Susan', into which they put their canvases and paints when they had the opportunity to go out. These expeditions were rare but very productive. Going up the Largo Road once, they came on a potato field in flower which gave Alison the inspiration for a very fine painting – once 'Susan' had been manoeuvred over the furrows to the right spot, and the work begun. Working outside had its trying side but could be amusing too. On one occasion Alison chose a subject where she thought she would really be free from onlookers and gratuitous advice. Then suddenly the children poured out of the village school and she was completely surrounded by them: all pressing round her to have a look. After a time most of the children drifted away but one little girl sat on watching with great attention. In the end she got up, sighed deeply and remarked:

'No! I'd rather be a missionary.'

When they couldn't go out, they took their cassette-player upstairs and played chamber music, which they had recorded from the Third Programme in the early morning, while they painted. It was no wonder that they prized the relaxation the music gave them, which helped their painting during the couple of hours in the early afternoon when their mother rested.

Next to the studio was a boxroom, full of cabin trunks and cases and hold-alls, hardly used since they were deposited there back in 1941. As it became clear that their mother could no longer manage the twenty steps up to the top floor, they gradually began to sort out what was there and to throw away what would never be needed. In this way they enlarged the studio and Alison had an area of her own with better lighting.

The RSA's printed records of the artists who have exhibited at the Academy, with the titles of their pictures and the years when they were shown, prove that both the McKenzies were having their work accepted every year during this time. In 1960, for instance, Winifred had three of her pictures hung in the summer exhibition and the same went for Alison in 1964.

Then in 1966, their mother died, ninety-three years of age, having lived in her own home to the end.

Friends of the RSA in Paris

Guide Vivienne Hamilton leads a party of Friends of the Royal
Scottish Academy outside the Louvre. On the left, Dr Malcolm;
behind him, Mrs Malcolm. On the right, Winifred.

13

Painting: Full Steam Ahead, 1966–84

After their mother's death, Winifred and Alison had to decide whether or not to stay in the Playfair Terrace flat. With fifty steps from street level to studio, with both bathroom and kitchen inconveniently situated and on the colder, less cheerful side of the house, they considered seriously the advantages of moving to somewhere more labour-saving. But then their ability to visualize how it might be possible to transform the layout, and take full advantage of the noble proportions of their drawing room and the sense of space the house gave them, made them decide to stay where they were. The wonderful stretches of wall space in their high-ceilinged rooms and on the stairs was another advantage, as was their nearness to the centre of town.

Nevertheless it was a major undertaking.

They stored their furniture and stripped the house completely. They took out fireplaces and blocked passages so as to create wardrobe and cupboard space: every feature they considered afresh. Alison proved to be the architect and Jimmie Gourlay, (the plumber), the clerk of works. The old kitchen was made into a bathroom off their bedroom, and their mother's bedroom became the new kitchen, facing the front and getting much more light. Here they were determined to make the very best use of space – no more having to put plates on the floor for want of flat surfaces! Units to fit two sides of the new kitchen were ordered from Dundee and a stainless steel sink and draining board and a new electric cooker.

A hair-raising crisis blew up with the arrival of these kitchen units from Dundee: the corner unit was just too wide to go through the front door. The delivery men were quite prepared to dump the furniture in the front garden and go: but the garden didn't belong to

the McKenzies. Jimmie Gourlay and the man fixing the telephone
were the only workmen in the house, but Jimmie took command.
He removed the kitchen window – luckily the space thus made
was just that much wider than that of the front door – and then
sent out some sort of SOS with so effective a magic that workmen
from all over the town – or so it seemed – converged on the flat.
They put up ladders and proceeded to heave the unit up. As it
got to the point where its weight was being shifted from the
men below to those directing it through the window, they heard
the cry:

'Watch! Watch! It's slippin!'

They could hardly bear to look. But mercifully all was well; the
men got it safely in and the McKenzies found sherry with which
they could all celebrate. After three months of chaos and turmoil,
their new home was finished and they were able to go on a planned
holiday to Vevey.

Painting could now take over.

Up to this point, the need to look after their mother meant they
could only rarely paint landscapes: they had had to concentrate
on still-life subjects and flower paintings. They now found, in
landscape painting, new impetus and fresh inspiration. They also
found very positive stimulus in the many fine exhibitions which
came to Edinburgh. All the great modern French artists had their
impact on them through these exhibitions: Cézanne, Braque, Dufy,
Chagall, Renoir . . .

When they had completed a number of paintings, it was their
habit to bring them down, duly framed, put them in a semi-circle,
sit back from them and consider what were the strengths and
weaknesses of these particular pieces of work. For these assessment sessions, they collected together and wrote down what they
had learnt from their own experience and from that of artists
they respected. To take some of these points from Braque (for
example):

'Scientific perspective is a ghastly mistake: it forces objects in
a picture to disappear away from the beholder, instead of bringing
them within his reach as a painting should.' And again, 'Every

new picture is an adventure into the unknown. It seems to me that I "read" my way gradually into a canvas. I never know how a picture is going to develop . . . '

Most of the observations, however, are their own. There is much emphasis on how to achieve impact:

'See with how little you can say how much.'

Another time they put in capital letters:

DON'T COPY NATURE.
SHE GIVES IN EXCESS.
SELECT.

And elaborating this theme:

'Art is *not* what a man sees, but is what a man *does* with what a man sees'.

Then there are direct reminders of their own practice:

'From time to time, lay down all your brushes (i.e., your craft). Look again at your canvas . . . and see if the picture is beginning to take control, whether parts of the painting are now nothing to do with it.'

Again:

'Eliminate unnecessary painting which takes away from the impact.'

There are the results of practical observation:

'Crimson plus transparent gold ochre = lovely deep red.'

'Line begins a picture and then ends it by making clear again design or meaning.'

'Rather let lines be too thick than too thin: i.e., suggesting a receding plane or cast shadow – not a wire!'

'Keep your colour IN your picture; watch that by being too strong near the frame, it doesn't pull you out.'

Both sisters were now working to their own timetable and according to their own lights. Alison, with all her things round her in the former boxroom, once remarked to Winifred:

'I don't think I've ever been happier!'

But there were also, for Alison, times of frustration and depression when she was struggling to find the right medium for new concepts. Each sister seemed to know instinctively, as an artist, what the other needed. All through their lives, Winifred would sustain and encourage Alison in her periods of self-doubt. In the seventies, she was developing her own individual and very difficult technique, using emulsion paints with water colours. It gave her the texture she wanted, gouache being too heavy. She always used frames with button backs which meant that when she had lived with the painting for some time, she could take it out and alter it – and many alterations in tone or design were made.

In a ledger both sisters kept a record of pictures sent in to exhibitions, also of sales, together with the names and addresses of purchasers. In many cases, when the pictures had been sent back unsold, they destroyed them. They didn't want to show them again, the frames would come in useful and storage space was at a premium. Alison called this 'defrocking', and having torn up her watercolour, would use the frame for another. Winifred found there were advantages in working on a scraped canvas or on one on which she could use the existing colour as the foundation for a new picture.

Neither of the McKenzies felt any need or desire to 'swim with the tide' in Scottish artistic circles. It is significant that Albert Garrett in his *History of Wood Engraving* wrote of the 'St Andrews School' of engravers, in that this suggests that the McKenzies, Jozef Sekalski and Annabel Kidston could be grouped together as being distinct from mainstream modernism. But it is also a misleading label in that each of these artists had already developed his or her own highly individual style, before circumstances brought them together in the 1940s and '50s.

Winifred and Alison, close as they were as sisters, had very different starting points as artists. Winifred brought this out in an interview with Linda Saunders, which appeared in *The Green Book*:

'In her own work', Winifred said, 'it was always light itself, flooding through trees for example, which inspired her. She started, heart beating fast, from the seen world.'

Alison was different:

'It started in her head. In Alison's work light illumines the sculptural properties of the subject: against the vigorous movement in "The Cod and Lobster" she sets this feeling of roundness and solidity.'

They were now free to contemplate holidays together and loved every aspect of them. Planning during the winter months was both the greatest fun and a serious undertaking in the sense that they looked up atlases, maps, travel books, timetables, guides – everything they could lay their hands on about their proposed destination. They went under their own steam, made their own arrangements and kept well away from the beaten track. Generally the choices they made for their painting proved successful but on one occasion they had to invent a pressing invitation from Violette in Vevey in order to escape from a place which was in every way uncongenial.

Another time, after Winifred had had a serious operation, Alison insisted that she should choose where they would go. She remembered a strikingly situated bridge they had glimpsed on an earlier visit to Switzerland. They tracked it down to Intragna, west of Locarno, but when they arrived there was no sign of the bridge. It was a beautiful place, however, and the mystery of the bridge was solved on one of their walks when they discovered its remains – the victim of floods, they supposed.

Up to 1975 their holidays were mostly spent exploring Switzerland in the company of Violette and from the first they loved the stimulus to painting that the scenery provided. Sion was their centre another year, chosen so that they could explore the upper reaches of the Rhône. From there they had planned a visit to Ovronnaz further up into the mountains. But they had to keep putting it off because of the weather. On the *last* day of their holiday, the wind shifted, the clouds began to disperse and, by the earliest bus, they made it up into the mountains. They had found they could spend the day up there and return by the last bus, the mail bus. From Ovronnaz they walked up the valley as the sun came out, which provided Winifred with a dramatic image, made up of retreating storm clouds, grey glacier, varied light on the different planes of the mountain sides and in the foreground, green fields and a clump of trees, brilliantly illuminated. She worked it up later in their St Andrews studio – a perfect example of 'emotion recollected in tranquillity'.

In 1975 it was Winifred's seventieth birthday and they decided to try something different: a cruise in the Mediterranean on the 'Uganda', with their cousin Margaret Cresswell. They started from Venice – and that visit gave Alison the inspiration for one of her mostly brilliantly designed and beautifully executed water colours, subdued in tone, quiet and meditative in mood.

This cruise then gave them the desire to explore Greece, whose landscape in its turn provided a whole new range of images: olive groves; Byzantine churches; jagged coastlines. These holidays, organized by 'Town and Gown' for people particularly inter-ested in flowers and birds, also provided opportunities for the McKenzies to meet congenial people and make (and keep) new friends. But old friends shared their holidays too: Hugh and Isabel Douglas, and Diana Pearson; George and Irene Caithness; and Margaret McGaw and Margaret Cresswell, for example, who went with them to Switzerland.

Then across this pleasant and creative pattern of their lives came the shock of Alison's sudden death in 1982 from a heart attack. The sisters had been so close and the blow so sudden that it left Winifred deeply wounded, needing to call on all her resources of courage and faith. She decided that the first thing she must do was to arrange a memorial exhibition of Alison's work. This was held in December 1983 in the gallery of the English Speaking Union in Atholl Crescent in Edinburgh. It meant a lot of work but it gave a focus to her life at this stage and the response of the McKenzies' wide circle of friends and of all who had the opportunity to see the full range of Alison's work for the first time made it worthwhile, as did the review which Edward Gage wrote for the *Scotsman*. It was a valuable assessment and is quoted here in full:

An important memorial exhibition of the work of Alison McKenzie (1907–82) is being held at the English Speaking Union Gallery, Atholl Crescent . . .

Born in Bombay, she studied design at the Glasgow School of Art and wood engraving in London during the 1930s, when she also received commissions for railway posters. Since 1940, when they settled in St Andrews, she and her sister, Winifred, have quietly and modestly yet significantly enriched Scottish art and, in particular, the cultural life of East Fife and Dundee, in whose college of art they taught and established the department of printmaking.

Their work typifies standards of excellence both in performance and pictorial organization. They are almost alone in Scotland in the way they gradually developed a very personal but recognizably post-Cubist emphasis on formalized structure, without ever losing a sensitive response to mood or atmosphere.

Looking at a cool still life of the late 1960s by Alison McKenzie, for instance, one senses the application of an intellectual process of analysis and synthesis which, in fragmentation and reassembling of planes, its desire to simplify subject matter, clearly derives from Cubism.

Tracing the growth of this approach is made possible in this delightful retrospective show and, though deliberately light-hearted and illustrative, some decorative panels prove she was already a past-mistress of formal organization at the age of twenty-three. In splendid LNER posters for the Yorkshire Dales and Norfolk Broads, the same ability brings lyrical landscapes to order, thereby displaying a graphic talent that blossomed in the brilliant engravings of the equivalent period in which idyllic features are inventively translated through rich variation of texture into designs whose underlying framework is as tough and resilient as any Constructivist resolution.

Although she painted in oil – a superb 'Snow and Sunshine: Gruyères' (1936) suggests relationships with the American artists, Hopper or O'Keefe, and a very formal 'Still Life with Fruits' (1953) is the first intimation of her post-Cubist treatment – she preferred the softer colours of water colour and gouache. Initially she used these thinly to create atmosphere as much as structure but she soon thickened it to body colour to fashion decorative synthesis of still life and town or landscape material – which she first introduced as elements viewed through a window beyond jug or plant forms.

At first too, such arrangements were hermetic and flat but in later compositions she reconsidered the tensions between objects in space. Spare but sensuous, quiet but vibrant, her paintings are Classical in their insistence on pictorial order while her choice of themes also proposes Classical associations – still life includes the ritual of urn, grapes and ivy; landscape often considers aspects of Greece, 'Corfu Cliffs', for example, is one of her most vital and dramatic images.

Always fresh, various, impeccably resolved and immaculately designed, Alison McKenzie's poetic vision will remain a special joy.

(*Scotsman*, 8 December 1983)

The interest aroused by the exhibition of Alison's work made Winifred's friends press her to consider mounting a retrospective show to illustrate her own, over the same fifty years. She went ahead and organized the exhibition, again in the gallery of the English Speaking Union, in April of 1984. Both exhibitions depended on the courtesy of the owners of the pictures lending them for these shows. In the event, they both proved wonderful opportunities for life-long friends, who made up an ever-widening circle, to salute the work of both sisters and for the wider public to realize what dedication to their art had been revealed.

Edward Gage, in his review of Winifred's work, wrote in the *Scotsman*:

Though fifty years of activity are celebrated here, most of the paintings come from the last two decades.

Early colour woodcuts and wood engravings – the superb 'Houses, Hampstead' is brilliantly laid out and enlivened with descriptive texture – are not only exquisite and typical of the period (1930–45) but demonstrate the endorsement of an emphasis on structural design which, as in her sister's case, was to inform all her imagery. Some early still-life canvases are darkly sensuous but the 'White Jug and Corn' (1973), where explosive arabesques are contained by a rectangular discipline, is an archetype of her mature vision of such subjects.

A similar analysis of formal structure underlies her landscapes wherever she finds them – in Crete, France or Fife. She can so order the 'Jungfrau' for instance, as to bring its majesty within her – and therefore our – pictorial comprehension, or she can successfully research a straggling olive grove for its essential masses and rhythms. Though order prevails magnificently, it never precludes lyricism in the communication of mood or place.

(*Scotsman*, 16 April 1984)

After those two major efforts of organization, Winifred resumed her painting – and her holidays. Increasingly she went with the Friends of the RSA, with whom she discovered France. A cruise with Isabel Douglas, up the Rhône, starting at Avignon, was the inspiration for a number of oil paintings. Looking from her cabin, she was thrilled with the light on Châteauneuf-du–Pape, with the brilliant blue of the bow wave in the foreground. Further north, when they had been through many locks on to the Saône, she painted, in evening light, poplars reflected in the quiet waters of the river. There were visits with the Friends to Paris and Giverny: Roussillon and Carcassonne, the Côte d'Azur, . . . and always with such congenial company. Each holiday was looked forward to as a meeting of friends as well as an exploration and an artistic adventure.

At the age of ninety Winifred accepted that there could be no more holidays abroad. Her failing eyesight also made painting impossible but she remained full of gratitude for those holidays and the inspiration they gave to the work of herself and a much-loved sister.

Appendix: Books For Reference

Further reproductions of the work of both sisters can be seen in the starred titles below, as also in the illustrations in the catalogues of Alison's memorial and Winifred's retrospective exhibitions which were held in the English Speaking Union Gallery, Edinburgh, in 1983 and 1984 respectively.

* *A History of British Wood Engraving*, Albert Garrett, Midas Books, 1978.

* *Shall We Join the Ladies? Wood Engravings by Women Artists of the Twentieth Century*, Studio 1 Gallery, Oxford, 1979.

* *The Green Book*, Special Scottish Edition, 1986

* *Scottish Water Colour Painting*, Jack Firth, Ramsay Head Press, 1979.

* *The Students' Book of Wood Engraving*, Iain Macnab, R.O.I., R.E., 1938.

* *Studio Magazine*, special number of *Image Magazine* devoted to wood engravings, June 1951.

See also:

The Dictionary of Scottish Painters 1600–1960, Paul Harris and Julian Salsby, Canongate/Phaidon Press in association with Bourne Fine Art, 1990.

Scottish Art 1460-1990, Duncan Macmillan, Mainstream Publishing, 1990.

References for Glasgow architects and the 1888 Exhibition:

Glasgow's Great Exhibitions, Perilla Kinchin and Juliet Kinchin, White Cockade, 1951.

Architecture of Glasgow, Andor Gomme and David Walker, Lund Humphries, London, in association with John Smith & Son, 2nd edition, 1987.

The Builder, Vol. 54, 1888, February, May August, October, November.

LIST OF PLATES

From originals all in colour, except Plate XV.

By George McKenzie

I. 'Green Landscape'. Oil. Date unknown.

II. 'Fishermen's Huts', Sewree, Bombay. Oil. Date unknown.

By Winifred McKenzie

III. 'Loch Gair', colour woodcut, 1935.
   Reproduced by courtesy of 'Arts in Fife', Fife Council.

IV. 'Devon Valley', colour woodcut, 1937.
   Reproduced by permission of Perth and Kinross Council,
   Museum and Art Gallery, Scotland.

V. 'Châteauneuf-du-Pape', oil, 1992.

VI. 'Sky and Bay' (St. Andrews), oil, 1985.

VII. 'The Tree', oil, 1991.

VIII. 'Tree Shadows, Lade Braes', oil, 1995.

By Alison McKenzie RSW

IX. Nursey Panel, originally in colour, 1934;
   illustrating the old rhyme:
   There was a man
   And he had naught
   And robbers came to rob him...

X. 'Yorkshire Coast', matt oil, 1936; poster for the L.N.E.R.

XI. 'Venice', watercolour, 1976.

XII. 'Fig and Monemvasia', watercolour, 1981.

XIII. 'Roadside Greece', watercolour, 1981.

XIV. 'Corfu Cliffs', watercolour, 1976.

XV. 'Cod and Lobster' (Staithes), wood engraving, 1936.

I. 'Green Landscape' by George McKenzie.
Oil. Date unknown.

II. 'Fishermen's Huts', Sewree, Bombay, by George McKenzie.
Oil. Date unknown.

III. 'Loch Gair', colour woodcut by Winifred McKenzie. 1935.
Reproduced by courtesy of 'Arts in Fife', Fife Council.

IV. 'Devon Valley', colour woodcut by Winifred McKenzie. 1937.
Reproduced by permission of Perth and Kinross Council,
Museum and Art Gallery, Scotland.

V. 'Châteauneuf-du-Pape' by Winifred McKenzie. Oil. 1992.

VI. 'Sky and Bay' (St Andrews) by Winifred McKenzie. Oil. 1985.

VII. 'The Tree' by Winifred McKenzie. Oil. 1991.

VIII. 'Tree Shadows, Lade Braes' by Winifred McKenzie.
Oil. 1995.

IX. Nursery panel by Alison McKenzie. 1934.

X. 'Yorkshire Coast' by Alison McKenzie.
Matt oil. 1936. Poster for the L.N.E.R.

XI. 'Venice' by Alison McKenzie.
Watercolour. 1976.

124

XII. 'Fig and Monemvasia' (Greece) by Alison McKenzie.
Watercolour. 1981.

XIII. 'Roadside Greece' by Alison McKenzie.
Watercolour. 1981.

126

XIV. 'Corfu Cliffs' by Alison McKenzie.
Watercolour. 1976.

XV. 'Cod and Lobster' (Staithes) by Alison McKenzie.
Wood engraving. 1936.